WAY *of*
Tarot

WAY *of*
Tarot

Evelyne Herbin
and Terry Donaldson

Thorsons

Acknowledgements

Many thanks and a tip o' the old hat to the following: Peter Pracownik, co-creator and artist for the Dragon Tarot deck and also 'Wyvern – the Game of Dragons, Dragon-Slayers and Treasure', both published by U.S. Games Systems Inc; to Stuart Kaplan, Chairman of U.S. Games for his massive contribution to the Tarot over the last thirty years; to Fiona Brown, Michelle Pilley and Michele Turney, our editors at HarperCollins; and all the participants in the work of the London Tarot Centre who have made this process of creation such an enjoyable experience.

Thorsons
An Imprint of HarperCollins*Publishers*
77–85 Fulham Palace Road
Hammersmith, London W6 8JB
The Thorsons website address is: www.thorsons.com

First published by Thorsons as *Principles of Tarot* 1996
This edition published by Thorsons 2001

1 3 5 7 9 10 8 6 4 2

A catalogue record for this book
is available from the British Library

ISBN 0 00 711018 9

Printed and bound in Great Britain by
Martins the Printers Limited, Berwick upon Tweed

Contents

Chapter 3
Meditation With the Tarot 180

Chapter 4
Where To Go From Here 190

INTRODUCTION

Historical
and Mystical Background

The earliest surviving Tarot deck comes from fourteenth-century Italy, where an Italian nobleman had a deck hand-painted as a present for his daughters' marriage. The cards were – and still are – a game: known on the continent as tarocchi, it is a game of numbers, where each card has a value, and the holder of the highest hand wins.

There has been a great deal of study and debate over whether the mystical symbols and religious themes shown in the cards were deliberately placed there by certain esoteric teachings, or whether – as seems more likely – they came into it as part of a process rather than a deliberate decision.

They show the major themes of life. They show what we can learn about ourselves. Each card is called Arcanum, which means 'mystery', but I prefer to think of them in terms of 'explanation': a mystery is something which cannot ultimately be known; an explanation enables us to live our lives with greater awareness, and therefore greater potential for happiness.

It is not so much what is 'in the cards', as what we ourselves are able to see in them. Depending on our own knowledge, we will see representations of legends, tales from mythology, hints at 'secrets', and explanations of them as well.

To work with the cards is a bit like going to the gym – it will enhance whatever is latent within each individual, depending on the amount of effort and actual work done.

Sometimes people ask, 'Don't you have to be psychic in order to read the cards?' The true answer is that by working with the cards, you will bring out your psychic potential, and activate it far more than you can imagine at this time. Thus, working with the cards will enable you to become far more intuitive about life in general, and more perceptive about yourself and others.

Working with the tarot isn't necessarily the same thing as reading cards for other people. By 'work' we mean using the symbols as sets of triggers to enable ourselves to make fresh realisations about our lives. The Tarot is really a set of windows through which we can look at life from a different perspective. One aspect of this work may involve laying the cards out for yourself, or for others, but not necessarily so. Even using the symbolism of the cards for your own meditations will bring about powerful results.

How to Select a Deck

It will be helpful for you to get a Tarot deck at the outset of your studies. It is important to select a deck that is right for you. There are many, many decks on the market these days, which is good in one way as it gives people more choice, but too much choice can be a problem for the beginner; when you first enter the domain of the Tarot you will see hundreds of decks, so you may well wonder where to begin.

It is important to avoid anything that is too specialised. There are many 'cultural' Tarot decks, based around Native Americans, wild animals, herbs or specific themes, such as the Celts, Arthurian legend, and the Vikings. Once you have a good grasp of the symbolism of the Tarot, you can move on and deal with the specific imagery of any such deck. You should have a good look round, and select a deck that seems 'right' for you. Make sure that the deck has pictures for the 'minor' Arcana cards, as well as those in the 'major' Arcana; otherwise it will mean a major block to learning their meanings, and you will be forced to rely on a massive amount of memorisation. In those decks where every card bears a picture, you can easily see what is going on and start linking the cards together. When you are ready, you might even like to have a look at my Dragon Tarot deck, which draws upon the world's symbolism of the dragon, from many different historical and mystical backgrounds.

Another point is that you should definitely throw away the little booklets which accompany each new Tarot deck. They are some-times written in a very negative light which only puts the recipient 'at effect', rather than empowering them to become more 'at cause' over life. Also, if you have tried learning the Tarot from some of the other very serious books on the subject, put them away also. You will find yourself able to get so much more out of them if you leave them alone and concentrate on this book for the moment instead. One thing at a time.

A good deck to start with would be the Rider Waite or Morgan Greer. The latter is the one I have used for years in training people. If you already have a working knowledge of tarot, then you may well like to get the Dragon Tarot deck, and see what what this has to offer you.

Getting Started

When you open the deck, do it in a respectful way. You could light a candle, and let opening the pack be a 'consecrated' act. Some people like to rub a little essential oil into their new cards. Whatever method you choose, try to let your entry into the domain of the Tarot be a special experience.

Make friends with all the inhabitants of your deck – you will be getting to know each and every one of them very well indeed; they will be guiding you on the adventure ahead into this realm of new discovery!

The purpose of the tarot is to help you grow as a person, so that the things which used to be problems in your life no longer trouble you, and the things which are holding you back at the moment will become insignificant as you continue to develop.

The more you grow, the more you will find yourself 'at cause' over conditions in life, rather than 'at the effect' of them. The whole purpose is to help you become more causative, to take control, and thus your life can expand in the direction that you want. Things that have been problems will become mere obstacles which you will be able to step over. Things that previously were out of reach you will be able to draw towards you. These are the indicators by which we know we are developing positively.

In this book, we are emphasising how you can weave the wisdom of the tarot into your daily life. This we will be showing you by meditations, etc. which we will be giving you to do. You will increasingly see your own experiences in the cards, and thereby bring the tarot to life. Its wisdom will become a part of your own life.

First we will be going through the meanings of the cards, starting with the major arcana, which follows the journey of the Fool towards spiritual fulfilment. I have described each stage of this Journey, card by card, and 'animated' it so that you can, if you wish, join the Fool along the way. I will then be showing you how you can link all the cards together in order to make sense out of the spreads which you will be doing for yourself, and for your friends.

ONE

THE CARDS
Themselves

The tarot is divided into two sections – the major and minor arcana. The pictures contain references to folk-lore, mythology, legends, characters from history, and provide us with lessons which we can begin to apply in our own lives.

The major arcana consists of twenty-two cards. When you lay the cards out for yourself or for others and any of these cards comes up, it will be showing the most important things that the querent (the person who is getting the reading; the 'questioner') is there to learn.

The minor arcana consists of fifty-six cards, which show the every-day situations, and the different kinds of people in the querent's life. Generally, the cards are laid out to give the querent an answer to a question. They may not have an actual question, however, but may be interested in getting an overview of their life from what the tarot reading has to offer.

The cards that indicate people are called the court cards. These are the kings, queens, pages and knights. They can show either situa-tions, or actual people who are significant in the querent's life at the time of the reading. Traditionally, the cards represent someone of the same sex, i.e. kings show men, queens show women. It is worth bearing in mind, though, that a king, for instance, could also repre-sent a woman who is in a position of authority, or heavily biased towards her masculine side, while a queen could represent a man who plays a nurturing role in the querent's life.

Here we are going to have a look at the individual meanings and associations of each of the cards. We are going to start with the major arcana, then go on to the minor.

Later on, we are going to show you how to do readings. Step by step we will show you how to make sense out of it all. The key thing is to enjoy it as we go along. Don't turn it into hard work!

THE MAJOR ARCANA

0

The Fool

The Inner Child

Man cannot discover new oceans unless he has the courage to lose sight of the shore.

ANCIENT CHINESE PROVERB

The Fool we see moving along Life's great road. He travels light, and meets new friends as he goes along. He carries nothing from the past, except for a small bag of tools, keepsakes and necessities. He looks towards the future without cares and worries, confident in what the future will bring, and confident about his ability to meet it.
You find yourself joining this character on his adventure. What do you want to get out of this experience?

Life is either a daring adventure or nothing! If we want to explore new territories and frontiers, the Fool challenges us to dare. Our lives are full of substitutes for real adventures. There is always an excuse or justification for inaction: we always expect somebody else or something else to entertain us; we play football in front of a computer screen; everything must be delivered to our doors. What's left to real adventure? If Columbus had stayed at home, he wouldn't have had the great adventure of discovering the New World! It is our mission now to go out there and seek our own truth and experience our lives as an adventure.

> According to the Fool, life is a game. The purpose of any game is to have fun! We can learn from playing. We need to do new things in life. We need to expand our boundaries. As long as we are content with our present situation – in every aspect of our life – we will not be interested in seeking out anything new.

The quality of the Fool needs to be directed, not repressed, as is too often the case in modern society. It needs to be provided with outlets. The role of the genius throughout history has been to awaken all the repressed earth-bound consciousness of his or her era, and to render humanity receptive for the new flux of ideas. Thus the Fool has always been an innovative or inventive figure, challenging conventional 'truths' and suggesting alternatives. He has always been ahead of his time. Genius has often been persecuted by those afraid of the changes it represents.

The Fool is there to say that we must emphasise our own individuality, not compromise it. He has an instinctive dislike of authority, and hates being pushed around by others. He needs a great deal of space to be himself. He hates routine, and wants to see new things happening around him constantly. He could easily attract partners who are erratic, unpredictable and incapable of commitment. His best characteristics are his dynamism and ability to dramatise.

The Fool possesses the innocence of a child. We must become as 'a little child' before we can enter his 'magical' kingdom. His intentions are pure. He is your inner child. You know, the one who is willing to make mistakes in order to learn from them! I could compare the Fool with a baby's first steps. In order to be able to walk, a baby has to stand up first. The baby falls down and tries again and again until it is able to find its balance and then, all of a sudden, the baby can walk. If we fail at something, we have to get up and try again until we can do it right. If we don't accept this challenge, we will soon become crippled in life and unable to stand up for our own freedom. The Fool learns from his mistakes. That's his secret!

His favourite tool is laughter. The Fool completely trusts what the universe has to offer. He has no fear. He does not worry about what he could have done or could have been. It is in the past. He creates his future now in the present time, not in the past or future tense. The past and future are excess baggage. He travels light, because he carries everything he needs in his knapsack! The Fool lives a simple life. **Simplicity is the key to life!**

Negative aspects of the Fool

erratic	irresponsibility	all over the place
naive	eccentricity	don't care anymore
elusive	embarrassment	don't show up
sliding	madness/craziness	out of control
rebellious	marginal	mid-life crisis
disabled	invisibility	unrealistic
stupid	recklessness	disruption
shocking	uncommitted	lack of focus

Key words of the Fool

foolish	versatile	fast reaction
enthusiastic	spontaneous	young at heart
unpredictable	novice	unusual/different

inventiveness	experiment	taking risks
revolutionary	innovative	reaching out
cheerfulness	drastic	element of chance
playfulness	exhilaration	freedom of individual
unexpected	eagerness	disagreement with the
		universe
festivities	fresh ideas	extrovert

Suggestions of the Fool

Break the routine.

Express yourself.

Cook something different.

Wear something unusual.

Visit a new country.

Explore your own village or city.

Talk to new people.

Be willing to explore new ways of thinking.

Keep your life simple.

Take a lively interest in all things.

Conquer your fears. Accept them. Fear results from the
    detachment of human consciousness from that of God.

Draw a caricature of yourself. Give it to a friend and ask what he
    or she sees in it.

Change your hair style or make-up.

Live your life every day as a new unit of time.

Don't rely on people's blessings (acknowledgement or agreement)
    to do your own things. Rise above it.

1

The Magician

The Alchemist

> *Your power is not in the middle nor at the end of an action, but at the beginning in your head.*
>
> ANON

> *The Magician stands at his table, demonstrating his skills and techniques to passers-by. He calls out to you to come and see what he is doing. You stop and go to get a better look. You find yourself astonished at the cleverness of this man. How does he do these tricks? Is it sleight-of-hand, or some greater power? You find yourself quite unable to explain it.*

The Magician teaches us about the role of communication, of developing our own ability to make ourselves clearly understood. We will develop through exercising our own minds and using reason. He is there to remind us to be on our guard against blind faith, or even overwhelmingly strong emotions. Study, and the training of our minds will give us the chance to develop our faculties in a systematic manner.

He shows us how to communicate, how to sell our ideas, how to develop abilities and craftsmanship, how to solve problems, how to juggle with different things at the same time.

Today's modern Magicians are in the world of media, press, advertising, salesmanship, etc. Indeed, they can be very persuasive with words or images in selling you anything!

Negative aspects of the Magician

too intellectual	cunning/sly	false facade
sceptical	academic	lying to avoid real communication
con man	compulsive communication	able to justify anything
pretending	coaxing	tendency to imitate
inattentive	inexperienced	acting all the time
absent-minded	volatile	always changing the subject
indifferent	nervous	too argumentative
indecision	make-believe	too changeable

Key words of the Magician

flexibility	discrimination	full exchange of beliefs and ideas
dexterity	details	role-playing
affirmations	potentiality	end result
performance	professional	information/ research
writer	self-determined	capable/able
intention	projection	language
dispassionate	logic	belief system
instruction	promoters/negotiators	concentration
agreement	thoughtful	international relations

Suggestions of the Magician

Learn to communicate effectively. Communication is everything
and everything is communication. Now look around
and see something or someone your wouldn't mind
communicating with.

Clarify your thoughts. Use the power of auto-suggestion or creative
visualisation to create what you want in life.

Commit things to memory.

Value knowledge and make use of everything you have learned.

Speak from your stomach (the willpower centre) not your throat.

Demonstrate your ability or skills/be competent.

Before speaking, fill your words with love and conviction.

Don't be a spectator of your own life. Play the leading role!

Talk to your neighbours.

When you read this card, think of yourself as a messenger.

Don't waste your time on silly arguments.

Learn to meditate, watch your thoughts.

Play some role-playing games.

2

The High Priestess

The Goddess Within

> *May your heart be pure as a crystal.*
>
> CHINESE PROVERB

> *The High Priestess stands at the entrance to
> King Solomon's temple of Initiation. She is the
> guardian of the entrance to this new dimension of*

> *experience that you are about to enter. In her*
> *hands she opens a scroll – the Torah – which*
> *is a symbol of the explanation of life and its*
> *mysteries. You are about to enter this Temple.*
> *What feelings do you have? Are you nervous? You*
> *should be, because your life is never going to be*
> *the same again! In the animation of this picture,*
> *she takes you by the hand and pulls back the veil*
> *that separates the outer courtyard from the inner,*
> *and thereby enables you to enter.*

The High Priestess is **the Goddess within**. She is the feminine principle, the Yin, the receptive side. She represents the intuition. She
shows us that the path to realisation is reached by overcoming our
own self-doubts, and by listening more trustingly to our own feelings and intuitions.

She is also synonymous with virginity or purity (the Virgin Mary, the
Goddess Isis). In this instance, virginity would be the symbol of
purity, i.e. in thoughts, feelings, desires, looks, words and gestures.

She holds sway over the water element. Think about it! Water is a
very powerful conductor in our lives. Our body is eighty per cent
water. Water purifies. Water flushes the kidneys, helping the blood
purification process.

There are two ways to clean or purify your system of all impurities.
The first way is to drink first thing in the morning, every day, on an
empty stomach, a cup of well-boiled hot water. The second way is to
sweat out all impurities once or twice a week in a sauna. Hot water
can get rid of many complaints such as migraine, fever, insomnia, etc. *11*

Negative aspects of the High Priestess

superstitious	doubt/contradiction	fears of the unknown
nostalgia	psychic attack	feelings are blocked
cold	uncontrollable fantasies	feeling mentally or physically impure
sacrifices	passive role mystification	sexual manipulation
cloister	feminism (fellowship of women)	not wanting to be known
puritan	mystery	

Key words of the High Priestess

common sense	good memory	receiving/picking
subliminal	duplication/reproduction	premonition
prompting	privacy	observing
time	soaking	information
empathic	neutral	fluids/layers
insight	sanctuary	deja vu/reminder
stimulus/response	matriarchal	subjective
knowingness	recurrence/pattern	clairvoyance/clairaudience
telepathic impressions	psychometry	myths and legends
impregnation/emanations	gestation/womb	energy fields
	channelling	

Suggestions of the High Priestess

Learn about flowers and gems and their healing powers.

Find out about the first priestesses or goddesses in ancient times.

Spend a day looking at the sea.

Purify your feelings and emotions.

Think first and then feel.

Do not intrude on people's lives.

Find out about psychic self-defence.

Hold in your hand a piece of jewellery. Empty your mind and see
what feelings or images come to your mind.

Find out more about the water element.

Ask and you shall receive.

Develop your intuition. Put some perspective in your life.

3

The Empress

Goddess of Love

*Love created the world and all the forces of
creation are subject to love.*

ANON

*The Empress sits on her throne, and welcomes
you into the garden in which she presides. Her
domain is over nature, and all forms of growth
and harmony. In the background are gentle
running streams, trees rustling in the gentle
breeze, and birds are singing. It is all very idyllic.
You feel the sunshine on your head and body. She*

13

*invites you to sit beside her in the shade, and as
you sit you feel the texture of the grass like a
thick rug. You see the symbol of Venus on her
shield, and realise that you are in the presence of
the Goddess of Love. She turns around and asks
you if you have a wish. What do you say?*

The Empress teaches us how to love. It is love that makes our lives
unfold and grow. Her sole motive is to love for the sake of love.
Perfect love acts without thinking of love. She is the Goddess of
unconditional love. Without her, everything will be dull and lifeless.
Instead of gloom and doom, she fills up our lives with feelings and
emotions; of joy, happiness and contentment. She is the elixir of
everlasting life.

Only love can bring things to blossom and prosper. The Empress
nourishes and fertilises the garden of our lives. She has understood
that the secret of life is love. Thus, she manifests and gives birth
to what we love, desire and nurture. She represents birth and her
beauty is incomparable. She is the Mother of all, Earth goddess,
goddess of fertility. She loves children, and all creatures in this world
are her children.

Love is manifest through the tenderest feeling, the gentlest look and
the sweetest words.

As opposed to the High Priestess, the Empress represents the physical (tangible) world.

The Empress is there to show us how we can learn about our emotions and feelings through self-expression. We may be very caught

up in sensual pleasures or, if not, we may need to be. We each of us need a great deal of affection from others, and acceptance. She shows how each of us is beautiful in our own right, without having to change. She reminds us not to react too negatively to setbacks in life, but to keep going. We must also learn to stand up for our rights, and be aware of when others are manipulating and exploiting us.

The Empress is associated with the planet Venus, sensual Goddess of love, harmony, unison, creativity and natural forces. She has a keen sense of aesthetics. She loves to express herself through music, love songs, poetry, arts.

Negative aspects of the Empress

too compromising	lack of assertiveness	neglect of oneself
too protective	timid	too sweet
relying on one's looks	plastic surgery	fear of getting old
buying love	love received with suspicion	dislike being alone
frightened by proffered affection	pity/sympathy	careless and unprotected sex
dislikes	fashion/beauty/ perfume industry	women's magazines that reinforce stereotypes
dependency	easily feeling hurt, offended and rejected	

Key words of the Empress

empathy	kindness/gentleness	wisdom
affection/	kisses and hugs and	hobbies

sweetness	cuddles	
family	charming	gracious
welcoming	reproduction	mid-wife
even temper	patient	pregnancy
harvesting	appreciative	friendliness
tactful	dedicated	abundance
gratitude	compassion	companionship
beauty within	a rose	self-worth
protective	selfless care and concern for others	manifesting

Suggestions of the Empress

Do what you always wanted to do (poetry, photography, etc.).

Learn to use herbs and plants for healing.

Learn massage/aromatherapy or reflexology.

Give back your talents to the world in helping the community.

Take care of your own area and the planet.

Give love to everything and everybody.

Listen to the harmonious sound of nature.

Be aware of the needs of your body.

Use your hands creatively.

Play with clay.

Be more in touch with nature.

Use natural products, make your own if you can.

Eat organically.

Flourish and prosper.

Tell your partner or a friend what you like about her/him. Do the same with someone that you don't like. Find out the good points in them.

Cultivate your creativity.

Redecorate your flat or house.

Design your own clothes or jewellery.

Imagine you are planting a seed. This seed represents a talent that you wish to develop. Intensify it with real images of you doing it. See how it feels. Then let it grow within you.

4

The Emperor

> *I did it my way.*
>
> FRANK SINATRA

> *The Emperor awaits your arrival. You enter his throne room and the doors are closed behind you by his guards. He has something very important to say to you personally, otherwise one of his assistants could have dealt with you. He leans forward and in a whisper tells you about a forthcoming battle which he must face. Will you join forces with him?*

The Emperor stands for leadership and self-determinism. He shows us how we can develop these qualities in our own lives.

To reach his position of dominion, the Emperor had to struggle for his own independence. He had to learn to be self-sufficient. He is the typical self-made person. He made some tough decisions, and conquered his opponents one by one. At times, he was hated by others. In spite of it, he kept his integrity, and gained full respect from his peers. Now, the Emperor is confident and assertive.

The Emperor is the representation of the modern warrior. His weapons are his good will and self-determination. He has earned his rulership by his own efforts. His kingdom is founded upon divine law and wisdom. He follows strict moral and ethical codes. Thus, he expects people to follow those rules too. After all, he represents order and self-discipline needed to accomplish anything.

The Emperor is there to teach us to develop through our own personal power. He teaches us not to be so reliant on others, but must rather follow our own instincts and impulses. Under no circumstances should we allow ourselves to become dominated or manipulated by others. We should be careful of compromising too quickly and easily in situations of conflict with others. The main areas we have to work on are our self-reliance and self-confidence. We will achieve happiness when we learn to value our own opinions and stand up for ourselves.

The Emperor represents the masculine principle, the Yang, the father figure, the patriarch. Like a father, the Emperor is here to instruct his children and to stimulate them to make progress. He can see objectively what is best for them. That is why he is demanding and firm. The greater the Emperor, the more demanding will be his teaching.

The Warrior Code of the Emperor is
Where ethics and morals are concerned, use your reason,
    be rational.
Follow a code of honour.
Be honest. Freedom is for honest people. No one can be free if
    they are not honest. If someone commits too many harmful
    acts against his fellow man, this person will soon be trapped
    in his own lies. It is only when a person has owned up to

and taken responsibility for his transgressions that he can experience relief from the burden of guilt he carries because of them.

Set a good example for others.

Be worthy of trust. Mutual trust is the strongest tie in human relationships. One has to demonstrate it to earn it.

Lastly, fulfil your obligations.

Now the Emperor is free from the effect of life; he is at cause. He teaches that freedom comes from taking responsibility. The Emperor is the master of his own destiny. He takes full responsibility for what he does. The more responsibility he takes over his own life, the more he is able to steer it in any direction.

Negative aspects of the Emperor

harsh	no second chance	overly severe
militaristic	too combative	can't listen to anyone anymore
excessive penalties	too vain	cowardice
mercenary	dictatorial	rigid
intolerant	suspicious	fear of losing control
too impatient	overly aggressive/ violent	extremist
rude	ferocious	unreasoning thrusts at danger
too domineering	selfish	bad tempered
rivalry	ruthlessness	imposing

Key words of the Emperor

heroes/heroines	perseverance	competition
power	sport	new possibilities
pioneer	brave	direct

headstrong	self-sufficiency	bossy
visionary	commander	pressure
powerful	self-assertion	motivation
purposeful	self-assured	muscular system
strength/strong	predators/hunters	vigilant
management	reliable	prompt action
ambition	inspiring/fierce	dare-devil
urgent	vigorous	

Suggestions of the Emperor

Try not to rely on anybody to provide everything for you.

Be industrious.

Keep your own counsel and select your own decisions.

Be true to your own goals.

Never minimise your strength or power.

Be brave and confront problems.

Develop your own line of work if you can.

Develop your vitality.

Practise some martial arts.

Never seek praise or approval or sympathy from others.

Temper your tendency for aggression.

Know what you have to know. Knowledge brings responsibility.
Responsibility brings control. Responsibility teaches us to
care, and to reach.

Make peace with your enemies.

Be a peace warrior.

Struggle for your own independence.

5

The Hierophant

The Teacher

> *Those who know do not say, those who say, do not know.*
>
> TRADITIONAL HERMETIC AXIOM

> *The Hierophant is the Grand Master of some secret society which you have stumbled upon. In the animation of this picture, are you going to join this secret group, or oppose them? Is what they are working towards good, or harmful for humanity? You make your decision, and the Hierophant reaches out and touches you between your eyebrows. Instantly, you feel differently about your life, you see that he is the representative of an ancient mystical tradition that has borne the light of humanity throughout many ages of darkness and suppression. You feel ennobled and special, to have been chosen to partake in the mysteries of a group so important to the history of the world.*

The Love of God is an unfathomable thing. This is the ultimate mystery of the Hierophant.

The name Hierophant comes from a Greek word *hierophantes*. It means 'one who explains sacred things'. In ancient Greece, he was the chief director of ceremonies and expounder of the doctrines in the mysteries of Eleusis. He was also called Mystagogus.

His role is to interpret and reveal esoteric secrets and doctrines. In Freemasonry, or in other mystical groups, he figuratively represents the Creator of the world, the Great Architect of the Universe. He is the Grand Master/Master of the Lodge figure.

Once upon a time, the Hierophant symbolised religion through the image of the Pope. Religion is a recognition of the link that exists between man and God.

Nowadays, the Hierophant doesn't have to be associated with dogmatic religious groups or sects. He is simply an intermediary (a link) between those seeking guidance and the Divine. Some people call him a Guru, Shaman, High Priest, or a Saint. He is here to show us how to grow spiritually. He is the Master Teacher, the Initiator.

Don't mistake him. He is *not* God, don't worship him as such (watch out for man-made Gurus on a big ego trip, or those seeking big financial profit). He is just a human being. He wants you to listen to him and to **put into practice his teachings.** Don't follow him blindly as if he were a pop star!

There are many different kinds of Hierophants around these days. Some may be doing good – others, well, you will have to judge for yourself! Some can be found running leper colonies, or behind the scenes with the homeless, the suicidal, the addicted. Some of these are the real Hierophants; they are teachers who do not even see themselves in any grandiose light. There are others: counsellors, therapists, consultants, etc. Some are doing a marvellous job, but some set themselves up as guru figures, offering a cure-all for everybody's problems but instead creating new patterns of dependency.

The Hierophant is there to teach us about compassion and charity. He helps others in a way that doesn't bring himself any direct benefit. He teaches us the lessons of persistence, loyalty, patience and perseverance in the face of opposition. Throughout the centuries and across the world, the teachings of the Hierophant haven't really differed. He teaches us to respect the faiths and beliefs of others. His most important teaching is that 'by their fruits ye shall know them', in other words, a person's actions will speak louder than their words.

The Hierophant is discreet. His motto is to be silent. His teachings are hidden, he is the power behind the scenes. He keeps himself to himself. He will only reveal his secrets to people who have merits. You see, the Hierophant doesn't waste his time on debate, he has nothing to prove. You have to seek him to receive him.

Negative aspects of the Hierophant

dogmatic	preachy	things can't be changed
autocratic	orthodoxy	cults/sects
too many charities	put on a pedestal	social position
celibacy	politics	theoretical
conformist	ungrateful	inflexible
immoral	patriarchal	hypocrisy
pressure groups	conspiracy	transmitters
chicanery	Mafia/Triads/ secret societies	indoctrination

WAY of

Key words of the Hierophant

hierarchy	philosophical	keys/scriptures
dream interpreter	revelation	communion
vocation	candles	sacred scriptures
community	benefactors	honours
fraternity	perpetual	ethics
builders	permanent	marriage
help/assistance	mantras	invoking
mage	respect	tradition

The suggestions of the Hierophant

Explore new beliefs.

Become a good listener.

Give people credit.

Make yourself available for charitable work.

Teach wisdom and love.

Find out about secret rituals in ancient Greece, Egypt, etc.

Think of your life as a series of initiations.

Create your own ritual, with some specific intention in mind.
> It could be a ritual designed especially to obtain courage, or to get rid of fears, or to banish a negative person or condition from your life.

6

The Lovers

Adam and Eve

> *Love is all.*
>
> ANON

You are in an open field and feel the warmth of the sunshine upon your skin. You notice that you are naked and in the distance you hear the sound of cymbals and flutes. You also hear the sound of human voices, and then see groups of people, some naked, some with garlands in their hair, making a procession towards you, drinking wine from animal skins and dancing and singing as they move forward. From out of the melee the most beautiful man/woman comes towards you. There is a sense of destiny as you look at each other. This other person is waiting for you to take the initiative. Are you going to become lovers?

In the Lovers card we come across the whole dimension of love, attraction, desire and sexuality. This is a big card! This card gets us to look at the kind of people we attract, and the kind we are ourselves attracted towards. Is there a type which we want to get together with? If so, what is it that draws us towards that type? The Lovers are there to teach us that love and lust are two different things, yet interconnected. The two lovers shown in the card are really going for it, unconcerned about whether or not their attraction for each other is acceptable to the conventions of society. Love – and desire – cuts across all social conventions.

This card teaches us to look at how we relate to others in the capacity of lover. Do we look after our lovers, or just use them, and then discard them? Can love grow from simple desire?

If we are experiencing a block in this part of our lives, i.e. we cannot find anyone to relate to in this way, what could we be doing to overcome those blocks?

Most of us want to be loved, but are we giving love to others? We will ultimately get back from the universe only what we are prepared and able to give to it. If we desire someone, are we being honest and up front and letting that person know it? And if they don't want us in the same way, can we handle that without feeling rejected?

This card is very relevant in getting us to look at our problems in love and sexuality. When we encounter an obstacle, do we allow ourselves to remain blocked, or do we focus on the intensity of our desire for fulfilment instead, and with the power of our intention blast away the obstacle? Many people remain unfulfilled because they are unaware of the sacrifices which have to be made in order to find love; they don't want to put themselves out too much, or they are afraid of hurting the feelings of others. In order to experience what this card has to offer we have to be prepared to pay the price. The theme of love – how it is found, how it is experienced – has been such a powerful inspiration for writers and artists through the centuries. But do the schools teach any of our young people how they can create for themselves better relationships, or improved communication and self-expression skills? Rarely.

The Lovers are also there to warn us about the dangers of sexual jealousy from others, and also within ourselves. It is the root of many of the terrible things done in the world.

Negative aspects of the Lovers

promiscuity	flings	seeking only pleasure
obsessive relationship	disliking the opposite sex	believing men or women are all the same
emotional dependency	tense	inconsistent
too flirty	inquisitive	too rational about love
criticising a lover behind his or her back	'love is blind' attitude	no trust
secret lover	imaginary lover	lack of commitment
infatuation	reading too many romances	too many expectations in a relationship
being manipulative	seeking out someone who could 'save' you	

Key words of the Lovers

anima/animus	mutual exchanges	good rapport
intense relationship	intimacy	closeness
considerate	comfortable	faithfulness
companion	emotionally secure	togetherness
enjoyment	friendship	same goals

Suggestions of the Lovers

Be more down to earth when it comes to finding a partner. Avoid the wrong meeting places (night clubs, bars).

Identify where you could find a suitable partner, someone who might share your visions in life.

Be willing to give and receive love.

Talk more openly to your partner.

When it comes to finding someone, listen to yourself.

Find out more about your lover before making a serious
commitment.

Spend a holiday together before the wedding.

Sooner or later, your love for your partner will be tested in various
ways, so as to measure the degree of your patience and
kindness. Have you passed the test of time?

Love yourself first before you can love, otherwise you are at risk
of attracting the wrong kind of lovers in your life.

Don't approach your relationship with rigid rules of expectations.
Be flexible and creative.

7

The Chariot

The Wild Horse

*The shortest way to do many things is to do only
one thing at once.*

HEARD AT CAMDEN LOCK MARKET,
LONDON NW1

*You are walking along a dusty road, and from far
away you hear the sound of a horse neighing. You
can hear the sound of a fast moving vehicle, and
suddenly, from round a bend, you see a chariot
moving at top speed toward you. The driver
hasn't had time to see you, let alone take any
action to avoid you. You dive to one side, and so*

> *narrowly miss the wheels of the speeding chariot.*
> *The driver pulls up his chariot and jumps down*
> *to see if he has hit you. He reaches down to help*
> *you back to your feet. You are a bit shaken, but*
> *otherwise unhurt. The charioteer says something*
> *to you. What does he say? Does he offer to help*
> *you continue with your Journey, or does he ask*
> *for your help in some way? Activate this scenario.*
> *See what happens.*

The Charioteer knows where he is going. Many people who walk around depressed or bored with their lives are in that condition because they literally 'have nothing to look forward to'; in other words, they have lost their sense of direction and don't know where they are going in their lives. They have lost sight of their goals. Thus, the Chariot card is getting us to define our goals. How can we ever achieve our goals if our mind runs wild in any direction at any time? Look at the gaze of the Charioteer. In which direction is he looking? Where is his future? Straight ahead! Where is his past? Immediately behind him!

A very powerful exercise is to sit down and close your eyes. Now where is your past? Where is your future? Is it ahead of you? That is where it should be, if you are forward thinking. If it is on your left it suggests that to get to your future you will be using more of the ana-lytical functions: reason, study, communication, verbalising, etc. If it is on your right it indicates that feelings, response, and intuition will be the vehicle or Chariot that takes you towards your future goals.

The Chariot card is there to say that you have to start by living in the present, in the moment. All of that stuff of the past will only entangle you. To reach your future objectives, the point where you can accomplish all the things you would like to see happening in your life, you can roll through the following exercise.

> *First, sit down and visualise all the things that you'd like to have in your life. All the love, abundance, fulfilment you can possibly imagine – and a lot more besides – is out there in the world, waiting for you to be ready to receive it. There is only one thing in life – and one thing alone – that can prevent you from failing to realise these objectives: and that is your own 'fence', or barrier.* **What I want you to do is put yourself there at that future point, and to look back at where you are now in your life. Now, as you look along the path which connects you, see everything slotting into place, creating the events which will bring you all you want for yourself at your future point.**
>
> *You don't have to put much strain into this. In fact, the gentler approach is the best. The subconscious mind reacts best when it is gently stroked, and definitely not when it is strained!*

When we look at the Charioteer, we are reminded of how simple things can be for us if, like him, we go straight from A to B. I once had great fun with a T shirt on which I had written the words, 'Come to the Point'. Wherever I went, people would start by talking about one thing, notice the T shirt, and then come straight to the point! They might ask me for something, or laugh, and then take the conversation off on a completely different track. It was very funny. It's not a bad idea to write out a sign like that and put it on your desk, or on your mantelpiece. You'll notice very quickly how people, when they see it, start loosening up and become much more direct. Being 'A to B' is refreshing, honest and liberating. Increasingly, both men and women are, I believe, becoming much more open and direct in how they relate to each other. Maybe that's just my own perception.

The Chariot card is also about borders, demarcation lines and barriers. Countries have borders, even if – as is increasingly the case in Europe – they are not manned in the way that they once were. People have fences around their gardens and psychological spaces around their bodies. There is the whole area of body language in which we can see how people cross their arms when they feel that others are encroaching on their space. They might also cross their legs, step back from near proximity with the offending individual, or purse their lips. There is even the expression, 'Good fences make good neighbours'. Without them, we start taking liberties with other people's space and this leads to friction.

It has been noted that the amount of personal space required by an individual is related to the population density of the area in which he was brought up. Those who were brought up in sparsely populated rural areas require more personal space than those raised in densely populated capital cities.

Negative aspects of the Chariot

moody	unable to complete any task	feeling under threat
over-protective	cruel	not allowing people their personal space
invading	closed	putting armour

distracted	grief	around one's feelings can't express one's emotions
disempowered	scattered in all directions	being pulled
rejection	overweight/ underweight	skin allergies
disconnected	emotional	worries
confusion	loss	lack of personal barriers

Key words of the Chariot

confrontation	purposeful	aiming
home sweet home	bond	mother-like
guarding	bodyguard	self-centred
Hara	fortress	layers
intentions	selective	tenacity
cherish	knowing what one wants	exploring

Suggestions of the Chariot

Buy proper clothing or lotion to protect your body and head from the sun or cold weather.

Insulate your house.

Make your space secure (home, car, etc.).

Every day, be reminded of your goal.

Define your roles or positions at work, at home, with friends, etc.

Learn to anticipate and avoid problems before they happen.

Draw boundaries when it is necessary.

Learn to complete tasks.

Focus on your goals.

8

Strength

Beauty and the Beast

Where there is no revelation the people cast off all restraint.

PROVERBS 29:18

> *We are walking through a wild mountain scene, in a jungle where the overgrowth has thinned out a little to make our passage easier. Through a clump of bushes we see a beautiful woman playing with a lion. The lion itself is huge, far bigger than any normal sized creature, but it is the woman who captivates our interest more. She seems to radiate a power of some kind. We wonder what to do at this point in our Journey. What do we do? Should we call out to her and introduce ourselves? Or should we just play it safe and continue on our Journey and hope that she doesn't see us? Activate this scenario.*

In some traditional decks, this card used to be known alternately as 'The Force', which somehow has a rather different association than strength. Strength suggests the ability to directly confront something and with power remove it. Force suggests something a bit more subtle. This card used to show Hercules battling with the Nemean Lion, as one of his twelve labours, which is quite a brutal

33

way of depicting this energy. Under the Ryder Waite tarot it is transformed into a woman of serene countenance, effortlessly opening or closing the mouth of a roaring lion. Above her head, a figure of eight Infinity symbol hovers. The purpose of the Waite version was to emphasise how reason should govern and direct the baser emotions of passion and desire. Waite's background was Christian and Masonic. He turned a very rough representation into a more gentle expression.

This card is first of all asking us 'What is Strength?' Obviously it is not just something which exists on the physical level, but mentally and spiritually as well. Strength can be defined as the ability to make change with our will-power. If we wanted to walk from the valley to the mountain top, we would need to maintain an awareness of our ultimate objective, otherwise we would quite easily get lost in the woods, or distracted, or choose some other point to aim for. People need goals. Without them, they become dispirited, depressed, and start feeling useless. There is no more effective way of disempowering people than by taking away from them the opportunity to do something useful in society. People are incredibly tough – they can work long hours under appalling conditions, as long as they feel that what they are doing is worthwhile. But when they feel that what they are doing is pointless, almost regardless of whatever money is involved, they will become unhappy. Children, for example, are very often discouraged by their parents from helping out with chores, and from taking on responsibility in the home. When this happens, the child may turn to crime, become rebellious, morose, moody. Through taking responsibility, morale rises; people feel productive.

This card is getting us to look at those areas in which we can effectively use our Strength, or strengths. Each person has different strengths. Some of us have the strength of convincing speech; some of enthusiasm; some of an artistic or creative potential. This card is inviting each of us to examine our strengths, and to work on them – by consciously digging them out and using them more. It is also inviting us to come together to pool resources. Gone is the old elitist Piscean-age notion that some of us are 'gifted' and others not. We have now entered the new Aquarian age in which each of us has a piece of the great Jigsaw Puzzle of Life, and the challenge is now for us all to unite and put the picture together. Each one of us can access the Collective Mind and begin downloading information and power from the source.

The Strength card is saying that we must prepare ourselves for what this new era may hold. Every so often humanity enters a new age. We once had the end of feudalism with the Industrial age, in which we saw the birth of cities on an unparalleled scale, the expansion of roads and railways, shipping, factories, all in a relatively short space of time. We have entered the Information age, in which information is the most important product, where news can be transmitted right across the globe over borders, past any censorship, through internet, cable, satellites, etc. All the old political and social structures are destined to change. We can each work with these new energies, or else ignore them at our peril.

There is another aspect to this card. It deals with invalidation. This is the minimalisation (making something smaller or less significant) of what we believe in. We must be aware when others are undermining us, either deliberately or unconsciously. We must never let this happen. We are all we've got, so let's value more fully everything about ourselves.

Negative aspects of Strength

lazy	aggressive	brutal and violent force of sensuality
body building	vanity	too hot blooded
impulsive	too big hearted	pompous
interfering	patronising	lust
showing off	uncontrolled sensuality	flashy

Key words of Strength

vigilance	merciful	indulgence
warmth/heat	generosity	combustion
courage	intervention	proud/pride
drama	creativity	challenges
willing and loving	vision	flamboyant
loyalty	sovereign	

Suggestions of Strength

Light a candle to renew your bonds with fire (spirituality).
Find out more about serpents and dragons or fabulous beasts.
Put your knowledge into action.
Develop your will.
Do a fire walk.
Link your head with your heart, and your heart with your will.

8

The Hermit

The Seeker

Sacrifice is the secret of every transformation.

TRADITIONAL HERMETIC AXIOM

> *We find ourselves moving along a long trail high into the mountains. For some time we have seen these mountains in the distance; now we are actually amongst them. We feel the cold, biting winds tugging at our thin clothing. How poorly we have prepared ourselves for this stage of the Journey! The air has become thin too, and we have to breathe more deeply to try and stay properly ventilated. It starts snowing and the light around us begins to fade. It is nightfall and we are lost in these hills, far from any shelter or sustenance. How distant seems any hope of survival! From the distance, though, we catch a glimmer of light. Is this one of the fairy lights about which we have been warned? We see it again, this time more consistently shining out there in the dark. Could this be a light being carried by someone? Shall we venture forth against the blizzard to look? Activate this scenario. What – or who – do we find? To what does he lead us?*

In looking at the Hermit card, I am reminded of the life of Milarepa, the Tibetan aspirant who spent a lifetime alone in caves, on mountain tops, in his search for enlightenment (the lamp of the Hermit). In fact, the Hermit is able to teach us much about being separate from the material world. We can lose sight of what is really important if we do not listen to him. We each of us need to go off every now and again and experience the silence so as to begin to tune in to that inner voice. Under these conditions, we can clear our minds of all the background noise which we have become accustomed to.

We all need as much to be alone from time to time as we do to come together occasionally. How often do we really make a point of delegating our responsibilities to others for a certain time and set aside for ourselves this valuable time? We need this space for growing, for nurturing, for being, for not 'doing' anything in particular. We are so used to feeling that we should be constantly 'doing', rather than 'being'. The original purpose of 'holidays' – or 'holy Days', as they were originally – was that people would be able to get this kind of time away from their normal reference points and landmarks.

A more problematic aspect of the Hermit touches upon the feelings of alienation and isolation that so many people experience. We have all been through these emotions at one time or another. Living even in major cities, people will rush out to nightclubs, pubs, bars, anywhere, to try and break down this invisible wall of loneliness which they feel. The teaching of the Hermit is to show us that such times need not be bad experiences: being alone can give us the chance to look more deeply within and to review our life, our feelings and our emotions. The world's greatest poetry, literature and music has almost all been created under such emotional conditions. Anything of greatness is born from the darkness of these emotions.

> *Criticism doesn't have to be negative all the time.*
> *You must try to be as constructive as possible if*
> *you disapprove of something or someone. If you*
> *wish to progress or advance in your work or life,*
> *constructive criticism can a very powerful tool.*
> *Be open to it!*

The Hermit is here to give us a helping hand. At some point in our lives, we all seek or need some kind of help or guidance. That is why the Hermit introduces us to certain practitioners at certain times. Let us appreciate those people who are truly dedicated to helping the world become a better place. What would we do without them?

Negative aspects of the Hermit

censure	being in the darkness	using people instead of serving them
shy/introverted	coldness	jumping to conclusions
	feeling like a	
narrow-mindedness	stranger	fussy
seclusion/alienation	unsociable	solitude
	perfectionist	alienation
worrier	unable to relate	resentful
isolation	to people	rejecting help
looking for faults		

Key words of the Hermit

appraisal	assessment	commentary
review	observing/looking	modest/humble
meditation/prayer	agile with words and hands	retreat
fasting	spiritual journey	thinker

39

writer	alternative medicine/ healing	meticulous
neat	withdrawn	industrious
order/method	selective	

Suggestions of the Hermit

Give a hand when it is necessary.

Do not harm a person of good will.

Look for the goodness in people.

Do voluntary work.

Before the beginning of any major spiritual undertaking, spend
   time alone, pray.

Learn to use your hands constructively.

Spend a couple of days alone in the wood.

Do not rush into new commitments, look before you leap.

Watch what you eat.

10

The Wheel of Fortune

Lady Luck

Think big!

ANON

*You stand before a great Wheel, which is slowly
spinning. This Wheel reminds you of the changes
in fortune which you yourself have gone through
in your Journey up to this point. It reminds you*

of the good times and the difficult times which you have been through. Now you can see how it all hangs together, like the different coloured threads on a single tapestry. You visualise yourself on this Wheel and can now feel more confident in dealing with any future problems which you may encounter on the road ahead, knowing that it will all somehow work out. Similarly, you now know that you will not be so elated when things work out well, as there will always be stormy periods in one sense or another that have to be gone through.

The Wheel of Fortune is an ancient symbol representing fortune and misfortune. The Wheel has many names: Wheel of Destiny or Wheel of Life or Wheel of Time. The Wheel raises many issues in our lives. We might want to know why some people appear to be luckier than others? What is our destiny? Can we change it? Or do we have to go through it all again in order to learn from it?

The Wheel is sometimes thought of as involving chance and is compared to the roulette wheel in casinos. If you actually look at professional gamblers playing, you will see that they are a very superstitious lot. They will suddenly move off from one table and onto another, if someone else starts playing that they don't like the look of. They will hover around, waiting for a sign or symbol to show them where to play and even how to play.

The Wheel is incessantly on the move. It is the Wheel which after all gave us mobility, wheels for chariots and tyres for cars and bicycles. With the Wheel, we can move from one place to another, from one situation to another. The principle of the Wheel is: nothing stays the same, we have to evolve all the time and move along with the flow. If you get stuck in one condition for too long, there is definitely something wrong, you have to see what you could change to move on to the next situation, otherwise you are at risk of going back to where you started from. That is why, in the fifteenth century, people believed that the Wheel of Fortune was merely the representation of: 'whatever goes up must come down'. It was a fantastic philosophy.

The Wheel of Fortune gives us not necessarily what we want, but what we need in order to progress. At times, it seems we haven't much control over it, we go through a different set of incidents or experiences which sometimes don't really make sense to us. In many ways, we cannot stop the Wheel, we have to go through it all. The Wheel changes the way we handle our fortune.

Good fortune can come to each of us in a number of ways. It connects with our own principle of generosity and givingness. It relates to our own bigness of spirit. It may seem as though some people are just incredibly lucky, but what we don't always see is how much work and intention has gone into the creation of whatever it is that has brought about their good fortune.

Faith is another aspect of the Wheel. Faith is the ability to bounce back after you have had a setback. Such a characteristic is comparable to that of a rubber ball. No matter how hard it is thrown to the ground, it will always bounce back. The harder it hits the ground, the higher it will rise again into the air.

The Wheel also represents faith in the future. Without any kind of faith in the future, people would stop having children, wouldn't bother with commitments, would run up huge bills. The Wheel reminds us that we have to think of tomorrow.

It was the invention of the Wheel which really triggered off the development of human society. For instance, the waterwheel harnesses the natural power of streams and rivers into a format for us to be able to use it. With this energy, we are able to grind corn, generate electricity, etc.

Many people go through the ups and downs of life as though they have their own built-in thermostat. When things start getting too good, their thermostat cuts in and shuts off the power. Then, after a period of cooling-off, their system starts up again and things start getting good for them. The reason for this is that when they get to the top of their cyclical progress, they start becoming arrogant, wasteful, they start misusing resources and become over extravagant. In their own innermost soul, they realise that what they are doing is wrong and the spirit within starts laying the groundwork for a period of scarcity to follow, in which they can get another chance to learn about the value of money, friendship, family; the importance of loyalty and the superficiality of material values. It has been said that 'pride goes before a fall'.

Negative aspects of the Wheel

overly optimistic	ups and downs	can't be bothered with details
setback	hiding behind destiny	drinking or eating excessively
roller-coasting	same difficulties coming again and again	big promises
forgetful of one's promises		diminishing

Key words of the Wheel

cycles	merry	opportunities in disguise
lay-back	believing	charity
big time	gift	sense of humour
test of faith	popular/sociable	abundance

Suggestions of the Wheel

Appreciate your good fortune: count your blessings.

Rejoice in the good fortune of others

Move up one step at the time.

Don't promise more than you can deliver.

Develop your faith.

Be moderate in everything you do.

Send blessings.

Be patient, have faith, work with love and help will come to you, from within and without.

11

Justice

The Law of Exchange

If one can work with opposite forces without going to extremes, one can really create.

ANON

You find yourself in front of a huge set of scales. From beside you a figure appears, hooded, prodding you to step into one of the pans of the scales. You feel a sense of trepidation as you do so. Something – you are not quite sure what – has been placed in the other pan, which is now being counterbalanced against you. You feel the upward and downward motion of the pans as they swing to and fro. You are uncertain of what this part of your Journey signifies. What will happen to you if the scales tip against you? Beside you, you can see strange shadowy forms, crouching in the darkness – they will be set upon you if you should 'fail'. Activate this scenario. What happens next? (Create it in your own imagination.)

Justice is with us at any time, anywhere and in all things. Justice stands for equilibrium. Justice is linked to the symbol of balance and to all weighing and measuring devices. If we do not add a little here and take away a little there to maintain the balance of the two scales, as it were the heart and the mind, unbalance will be the effect.

Justice may be defined as a form of commerce. To obtain something, one must pay for it. Justice is related to those simple and unimportant things that we take for granted in our lives. Justice is possible only if we give and take. **Justice represents the law of exchange**: you take something and you must give something in return. If you can make both sides of the scale balance, it is justice.

Justice is warning us not to abuse the rights of others. It teaches us the principle of ownership and to respect people's property. When one does not respect the ownership of things, one's own belongings and property are at risk.

To really understand Justice, we must look not only in term of material possessions, but also in term of our feelings and thoughts. If we put too much emphasis on wealth and possessions, we are slowly diminishing the need to develop our spiritual life. We are not hungry any more to read, or study, or meditate. It means we are no longer pushed by need. If we can accept that it is occasionally necessary to deprive ourselves of a little comfort, we will soon feel ourselves coming to life again.

There is no escape from the repercussions of what we have done. Most of the bad or negative things we have done in the past we have simply forgotten, but they lie there like dead rats under the floorboards, decaying and gradually emitting a smell over the years that becomes increasingly difficult to ignore. Cover it up with sweet-smelling perfumes we may try, but eventually the floorboards will rot away and our stable foundation will disappear, like a rug pulled from beneath our feet. So often in society we will do anything to hide a problem rather than confront the evil or neglect that is causing it.

Most of the 'negativity' out there is due to people trying to solve problems using destructive methods. People do need to have challenges to face and to overcome. Without such challenges in life, they will create their own problems, e.g. bad health, depression, aimlessness, drug addiction.

> *The Justice card teaches us about karma, which means that we will each be rewarded for the good we have done and punished for the bad. The process of karma may take time to filter through, but it is inescapable.*

Just like the karmic chain of cause and effect, so in nature there is another kind of balance: the food chain. Ecologically, nature is an incredible alchemist, turning natural waste into clear skies and water. It is mankind, though, who now seriously threatens nature's ability to cope.

Negative aspects of Justice

indecision	unfairness	too much power when it is not necessary
evil purpose	disease	seeing only one's own way
rewarding crimes	blind justice	man-made justice
disadvantage	propaganda	being blocked or
chaos	suffering	prevented from
prison	laxity when	helping
harshness when	severity is	karmic debts
compassion is	required	
required		

Key words of Justice

readjustment	diplomatic	moral/ethics
law/solicitors	code of conduct	prosecution
witness	guilt	bargain
trial	defendant	penalty
punishment	decisive	sentence

Suggestions of Justice

Report crime/oppose injustice.
Listen to everybody's point of view before making a decision.
Don't take sides.
Be objective and fair in your views.

Don't accuse without knowing the truth.

Accept your karma. If you manifest spiritual qualities such
as love, patience, sacrifice, goodwill, your problems will
be greatly lightened.

Make long-term plans.

When it comes to making a decision, weigh up the pros and cons.
You can use an imaginary set of scales to represent
either choice.

Seek balance and equilibrium.

Look at your own shortcomings (evil deeds).

12

The Hanged Man

The Submissive

*The truth is sometimes the opposite of how it
seems.*

ANON

> *You are walking through a forest and come across
> a strange sight. Hanging upside down from a
> small scaffold is a man, with his arms tied behind
> his back. You see a small sign pinned to the side
> of the scaffold, which reads: 'This man is guilty
> of a crime. He is to hang here for one full day. If
> anyone cuts him down or brings him sustenance
> of any kind, they will receive the same
> punishment as him'. The man is clearly suffering.
> What do you do?*

Back in medieval times, criminals were hanged upside down by one foot for the length of a day, from sunrise to sunset, as punishment for their crimes. Women who practised herbalism were given the same punishment by men, afraid of the power which they represented, the power of the unknown. The whole witchcraft scare was simply an attempt by male doctors to wipe out the opposition who were really doing nothing but practising an age-old form of healing and midwifery. The rope which we see holding the Hanged Man to his support reminds us of the umbilical cord, which at one time connected each of us with the rest of the physical universe. It suggests a further link with the Great Mother, the Sea. We are all the spawn of the same Mother.

The Hanged Man is a card which invites us to look at our hang-ups, our inhibitions which can hold us in fear and servitude. We don't **have** to play the victim.

Nothing much happens in the company of the Hanged Man. He just hangs around doing nothing, thus producing nothing. He stands for passivity. In fact, he is a bit like a weathercock. He constantly swings with the wind between comments, opinions. One minute he follows one belief and the next moment, another. His world is made of dreams. He likes to escape from it all. He is there to warn against being similarly open to every influence.

> *The Hanged Man is there to ask us what we are*
> *prepared to sacrifice in order to be able to move*
> *on in life.*

If you look at the shape made by the Hanged Man's arms (folded behind his back) and his one leg crossed over the other as he hangs upside down, you can make out the downward-pointing triangular symbol of Water. This is a very important element in our lives. Water is the most powerful of all the elements. It erodes entire continents and transports vast quantities of goods across the globe. Even now, the entire east coast of England is gradually collapsing into the sea, while the west coast is rising by about half an inch a year. It is the element water that cooled the earth after its creation and allowed life in its most elemental, amoeba-like stage. Water manifests in many forms: gas, solid and liquid. It is indestructible.

Negative aspects of the Hanged Man

impressionable	predisposed	malleable
resigned	too open	unrealistically idealistic
impractical	hidden feelings	too absorbed in one's own problems
careless	misleading	seeing the world upside down
pushed about/ rejected	unnecessary abuse	frozen situation
cloudiness	victimised	listening to gossips
elusive	living in fantasy	

Key words of the Hanged Man

obedient	suspended activity	period of delay
visions	mysticism	vapours
fog	waiting	transcend
unselfish	mist	stillness
nebulous	transition	delay
sacrifices		

Suggestions of the Hanged Man

Stop doing things to yourself if they are harmful.

Don't be swayed by the winds of public opinion.

Don't let your friends or relatives tell you what you should
do or think.

Stop playing the role of martyr.

Look for the truth instead of listening to gossip.

13

Death

Rebirth

> *Change is never a loss – it is change only.*
>
> BUDDHIST MEDITATION

*You become aware, bit by bit, of yourself standing
in a deep and very dark mist. You can't see far
at all but, shivering against the cold, you start
moving in a random direction. After a few paces,
you bump into a rollright stone. You realise that
you are in the middle of some ancient Celtic stone
circle. It is extremely silent. No sound penetrates
the thick fog which blankets the whole area. You
wonder how you are going to find your way out
of here. You consider the prospect of walking,
but have no idea how far the nearest civilisation
might be, or even in which direction it might be
found. You consider that at least it is better to
keep moving and keep out the cold air that seems*

51

*to be trying to find its way beneath the folds of
your cloak.*

*You begin walking, aware of the diverse
qualities of ground beneath your feet. Sometimes
the ground is hard, sometimes sandy. Now and
again you find yourself ankle deep in freezing
cold mud, which chills your ankles to the bones.
Time passes by, you seem no nearer to finding a
way through this mist, or the realm of darkness
from which it seems to emanate. Suddenly,
standing right in your path, you see the silhouette
of a human form, which seems waiting for you.
You are a bit frightened at this, but decide to
approach the figure to see if he can lead you out
of this mess. As you draw closer, you see that the
form carries a large scythe over his shoulder.
What happens now? Activate this scenario;
let it come alive in your imagination.*

Death is, in many ways, a commemoration of life! It is spring after
a long and cold winter. When spring comes, the earth is warming up
and new seeds and foliage can start to grow again. There is a sense
of renewal and freshness in the air. Animals, flora, fauna and human
beings come to life again. **Death is the symbol of rebirth.**

In many societies, Death is celebrated as a new freedom for the
soul. One has to realise that we are not only made of bones, flesh
and blood. We are primarily spirits incarnated in a most particular
shape called a human body. The body is like a piece of clothing;
after so many years of constant usage, it eventually wears out. Thus,
the body is just a vehicle for the soul.

It is extremely difficult for the soul to leave the body if the bonds between the body and soul are too strong. That is why so many people are incapable of leaving their body even at the moment of death. Because while they lived here on earth, they were only interested in their material existence. Death is here to teach us how to detach ourselves from the world of matter. In fact, the soul has no time to waste, she is here on a special mission, and once she is finished, she has to report her work to the invisible world. If her work is still incomplete, she will have to come back again and find another vehicle to carry on. All born into the physical world are limited to mortal form and therefore will in time die.

In the story of Dracula we see someone who can't let go of someone. Dracula became so furiously determined to see his deceased wife again that he hung on to his body for centuries, keeping himself alive by siphoning off other people's life force. His body became like a prison. Once he found her, his mission was over. At last, his soul could be free again from all sufferings of the past.

Every culture has glorified Death. The ancient Egyptians spent most of their national wealth on building the pyramids. In our society, every time we switch on the television, we see the glorification of shoot-outs, car chases and scenes of women being attacked. Murderers are celebrated. Books are written – and millions made – about the hideous crimes they perpetrate. The shattered lives of their victims and their families are as nothing. Those that do good are ignored or ridiculed. When a society gets into this state, it is a sure sign that society itself is dying.

This card also touches upon recycling waste products. Great progress has been made in recent years concerning the re-education of consumers through the campaign for greater ecological awareness.

People are recycling paper, glass and cans and are generally more aware than they were twenty years ago about the dangers from car pollution, hair sprays, chemicals and drugs in food and water.

The next stage is to get them aware to the point where they begin to exercise similar choices regarding the kind of entertainment that they are prepared to see expressed in the media. When people flatly refuse to passively watch scenes of gratuitous violence and mayhem, when they break the agreement with the media moguls that it is OK to transmit this stuff and the advertisers can't sell any of their products through their programmes, then things will change and we will begin to realise a better kind of society.

Death shows us how very destructive it can be to hold on to things or people or feelings. Thus, the Death card encourages us to let go of those harmful habits and to set ourselves free again to start afresh. Ask yourself: What do you have to lose? Or what do you have to gain? Start now. Every end is a new beginning.

Death is what frees us from the past. In the Reaper's hands is a scythe. When I worked on a farm, we used this instrument for clearing undergrowth, especially weeds. The scythe doesn't actually uproot them and thus permanently prevent them from coming back: it just clears the deck for a certain period. This aspect of the Death card is asking us to what extent do we ask for a resolution of our problems? Or are we just continually 'coping' and cutting off the tops of all of our problems, only for them to regrow and return to give us continued grief in the future?

> *You can use the symbol of the scythe to cut the bonds that bind you to the past: to people or harmful feelings. Symbolically cut them one at the time.*

Negative aspects of Death

draining	attached	selfish
jealous	spiritualistic seances	apathy
accumulation	putrefaction	toxic
irritable	devious	compulsive
addictive	poison	vindictive
bad-tempered	secretive	obstinate
obsessive	claustrophobic	impotent/frigid
can't let go	scandals	hostile
life insurance	threat	vicious
venomous	intolerant	forceful
undertakers	inactivity	

Key words of Death

resurrection	secret	orgasm
fantasies	enigmatic	determined
deep	metamorphosed	fascinating
pain and pleasure	tenacity	in control
horrors (films, books)	sensation	shift
release		

Suggestions of Death

When you have not succeeded at something, withdraw from it, study it and then try again.

When you give up a bad habit, replace it with a good one.

Don't be afraid to change.

Learn to cut your losses and move on.

Don't hold back dying relatives or friends, do not try to communicate with them. Let them go in peace.

Cut away old negative conditions to start afresh.

14

Temperance

The Perfect Blend

What lies behind us and what lies before us are tiny matters compared to what lies WITHIN us.

Seen on a placard in a street

demonstration in India, 1978.

You stand upon an open road which lies before you, trailing off into the distance. As you move along it, you come across a pool of water to one side, which gleams in a peculiar way. You stop to look more closely at it and, as you look at your own reflection, a change seems to occur on the surface of the water. A rippling movement seems to cross its surface and after that you not only see your own reflection, but that of someone else standing behind you. You jump up, turn around and there before you stands an angel, with a powerful radiance emanating from it. The angel holds in each hand a cup, with water – or what seems to be water – flowing in mid-air between them. The angel has come to give you a message. You struggle to speak, but cannot. Nonetheless, you do seem able to communicate through your thoughts. What transpires between you and this angel on this very auspicious day? Animate the scenario.

Temperance, as used in the tarot, does not have the same meaning as the word used by, for instance, the Temperance Society, which campaigned in 1930s' America for the abolition of alcohol. Here it refers more to the process of being tested and of refinement, just as a sword is tempered on an anvil before being polished up for sale. It gets us to look upon those experiences in life which have put us to the test and enabled us to become better people.

Temperance is really nothing more than an indication of the problems that we have to confront and solve in life. If we are able to purify ourselves, Temperance will manifest in terms of help 'from above'. It could be therapy, counselling, or some process of healing. That is why we must go through Temperance in order to clean and purify our soul of negative Karma. Temperance is a bit like a dirty windscreen: we need to clean it to see the road again.

With Temperance, we are recognising that we are born here on earth as rough stones. We are each precious stones still undiscovered. When a diamond is found, it is at first just a piece of stone, it is uneven, jagged and opaque. It needs to go through a series of different stages of work to reveal its beauty and translucence. The same principle applies with the soul. Temperance is like a crystal ball: it represents clarity.

> *Work with precious and semi-precious stones.*
> *Identify yourself with them, be like them.*
> *Meditate on their beauty, colours, purity. See how*
> *they capture light and reflect it. Ask them to give*
> *you all their properties and virtues.*

The Temperance card encourages us to develop our awareness of the truths which philosophy and religion have to offer. It is not saying that we should accept anything uncritically, but that we might find a great and unexpected source of fulfilment from starting to look at life from these perspectives.

It is also getting us to look at those things to which we give our support. Do we support our friends in positive ways, as we would wish to be supported? If we are unhappy with something, we must remember that we have the power to withdraw our support from it. For instance, if we are unhappy with the never-ending diet of violence and evil in the media, we should stop buying magazines and newspapers which promote them. Our money, our time and our attention are **votes** through which we can register our approval or otherwise for something.

The Temperance card also rules over healing and is there to teach us about the many different kinds of healing that are now open to us. Homoeopathy is now well respected as an alternative to orthodox medicine. Acupuncture, hypnotherapy, crystal healing, chakra balancing; how many of these have you tried? Maybe you'd get better results from trying something like this rather than running to the doctor to get a drug for the symptoms of whatever you are suffering from. If you haven't tried these, at least you should try shiatsu, for example. Find a practitioner of one or more of these therapies and let them get to work unravelling all the knots and blockages that you have.

Negative aspects of Temperance

stuck in the past	too delicate	afraid to be hurt
dirty	sensitive to pain	healers who need to be healed
nothing wrong with me!	refusal to learn from past traumas	looking for the easy way out

Key words of Temperance

new teaching	spiritual elevation	fire and ice
alignment	bridge	straightforward
lively	exploring	enlightenment
transparent	enhancing	brilliance
style	fusion	mission

Suggestions of Temperance

Cultivate your spirituality.

Practise self-healing.

If you can't do it on your own, join a support group.

Support alternative healing or practices.

In order to develop a greater state of awareness, one needs to look into the past to understand the present.

Place truth in your soul and you will acquire freedom.

WAY of

15

The Devil

The Joker

> *It is the guilty who point the accusing finger.*
>
> ANON

> *You stand in a dark hall that is lit by firebrands,
> their flames springing from bowls of oil which
> are suspended by chains from the ceiling. These
> lights give off little light. The air is chilly. You
> make your way down into a great hall which has
> no windows. You come to the foot of a grand
> staircase. On the walls to one side we see
> displayed various objects designed for
> punishment or penance: whips, branding irons,
> scourges, all intended to cause suffering through
> the sense of touch. Your foot slips on the blood
> that is spattered over the ground. From the
> ceiling a dull bulb throws off a yellow light. Down
> the corridor someone screams in agony. What
> happens next?*

The Devil represents all that is negative and seems to hold us back,
or are we just blaming the wrong things for our own lack of determination and success? Are these barriers real or are they self-
created to sabotage us?

The Devil card has much to do with lack of vision. People can get stuck in this card – as indeed they can in any other – only here it really is quite gloomy. People who are stuck in guilt are their own worst Devil. They punish themselves with illness, depression and impoverishment. Not financial impoverishment, necessarily, because the devil can allegedly grant money to his supporters, but something that is really akin to an inability to have things. People who make their money out of evil ways, drug dealing, prostitution, exploitation, crime, may well accumulate money, but they will never really enjoy what it brings them. Money acquired from sources such as these is a bit like 'fairy gold', which would seem to be able to solve problems when it first arrives, but in the light of the ensuing morning will have turned to dust. The happiness which they had hoped such money would bring them simply wouldn't be there. It is as though there is a curse on money made from such sources. The Devil card is there to remind us to keep hold of our ethical principles and not to compromise them, even if that means being ostracised by our peers.

The traditional representation of the Devil card was a man and a woman chained by a devilish figure. The Devil card is an illusion that one is trapped because, If you look more closely at the card, we can see that those chains are quite loose. Thus, most bondage is by choice.

The Devil works on the basis of guilt, remorse and self-abnegation. So many people condemn themselves for their past misdeeds. They go through their lives in abandonment and slavery, both sides of the same coin, and feel that life cannot offer them anything new or different. People addicted to drugs are the most obvious aspect of this chain. The Devil encompasses all aspects of compulsion and enslavement. He represents all those things which we have to let go

61

of. They may seem like pleasures at the time, but they only keep us imprinted with all of the old patterns of the past. 'Better the devil you know,' they say, 'than the Devil you don't.'

The Devil card gets us to confront our own negativity and suggests that we begin to look at ourselves more positively. We must really love and accept ourselves and not sit in judgement and be self-condemnatory. It is one thing to be complacent, but yet another to refuse to acknowledge your own beauty, strength and wisdom. Look at how wise you can sometimes be! Look at how beautiful you are! It is only *your* mind that says you are anything less than perfect.

The Devil shows us how we can choose to look at situations. Do we see them as fraught with problems and difficulties, or are we able to see them as opportunities in disguise?

> *If you meet temptation, injustice, contradiction, doubt or adversity, maintain your faith in the sacred fire which has been placed within you. Know that nothing and no one can extinguish it or take it from you.*

The Devil can also be very constructive in our lives. In a sense it is because of him that I have learned to appreciate life in full and gained the drive to go beyond my own limitations. I couldn't hide anymore under his domination: 'I can't do it', 'I'm stupid', 'it's too expensive', 'nobody likes me', etc. By confronting him face to face, I have found the best remedy in dealing with him: a good laugh. That's all it takes. When you can laugh at your own problems, you are halfway there.

Negative aspects of the Devil

ignorance	greed	envy
too much pride	narrow-minded	misuse of one's power
manipulation	hatred	suppression
false purpose	grumbling	pessimistic
self-defeating ideas	self-punishment	corporal punishment
imposing	pure selfishness	feel the need to test others
stubborn	need to dominate	will prove you wrong
invalidation	denial	disregarding the rights of others
rigid/inflexible	devious	perverse
complex/web	the accuser	vices/sadism
fatalism	misery	

Key words of the Devil

thinking	change of view	mirroring
accepting/tolerance	comparing	future
serious	respect	structure
prudent	calculated	conventional
hard-working	discipline	responsible
reserved		

Suggestions of the Devil

When you are in doubt about your actions, look at your own motivations.

Do not impose your views or will on others.

Do not punish for the pleasure of it.

Don't invalidate.

Learn to laugh at your own problems.

Be gentle with yourself and others.

The only force which has the power to vanquish evil is Divine love.
The principles of love harmonise all things. Learn to love.
Set yourself free from bondage by acknowledging your freedom
of choice.
Develop higher self-esteem.

16

The Tower

The Destroyer

> *You don't have to suffer continual chaos in order
> to grow.*
>
> ANON

It is night, but lightning fills the sky, for a
moment illuminating a very desolate slope where
molten lava has piled up and solidified into
grotesque shapes. From the distance you see
a high, cone-shaped peak, from which a dull
red light is reflected by some passing clouds,
indicating a volcano that is not completely
dormant. A cold wind moves around you, a biting
wind that stirs anger and hostility, even if there is
no cause. The clouds part and now you can see a
small building sitting on the slope of the volcano.
It seems to have been there for ages, so old is its
architecture. How has it survived the rumblings
of the volcano? You begin to move closer to it and
now can see that there is light coming from it and

that the inhabitants are singing some kind of hymn, or liturgy. Activate this scenario.

The Tower is here to challenge the foundations of our lives. Do we build castles in the air or do we build on solid ground? With the Tower, we can see the lightning striking the side of the building. Many commentaries have said that this represents God breaking down the work of man. What it shows more clearly is how God gets blamed by man for his own mistakes, because if the Tower had been built with a lightning conductor, it would have escaped destruction and the electrical discharge would have passed into the ground harmlessly. Similarly, in our own lives, we must take the responsibility upon ourselves if we want things to work out. We can't keep blaming our parents, our background, our governments, or our god(s): we have to take back our own power by taking back the responsibility. As long as we are stuck in blaming external influences we will be giving away our power and relinquishing any chance of change.

The Tower makes us look at precautions. If a house is built on sand, or the foundation has not been properly implanted, it is obvious that years afterwards this house is doomed to fall apart. If the owner or people around don't do anything about it, eventually this house will suddenly collapse into rubble, taking with it the neighbouring houses.

The same phenomenon occurs in our lives. If we do not make sure that the foundations upon which we build our lives are solid, the thunderbolt of the Tower will destroy them completely. We only have to remember a time when we have seen something rapidly destroyed to see the Tower influence at work.

The effects of the Tower are quite devastating. They could manifest as a chain of disasters (you lose your keys, then your car gets stolen, then somebody breaks into your house, then you lose your job, etc.), or as a nervous breakdown, an accident, an illness, etc.

The Tower card purges us of old attitudes and behaviours. It opens people's eyes to new reality. Every crisis detonates the illusions that anchor our lives. The Tower is in reality a stepping stone and lays new foundations in our lives. It is here to test our strength and help us in re-evaluating our present situation.

> *Life on earth is a great school in which we are constantly put to the test. It is by passing through a series of trials that people gradually develop faith, hope and love.*

This card is here to teach us about courage in the face of adversity.

This card teaches us about anger, yet anger needn't be destructive. If given a positive outlet it can be a force for bringing about creative change. It was anger that motivated people to abolish the slave trade, to fight for the Magna Carta or Bill of Rights and for the freedom to choose one's government. When anger is suppressed and given no outlet it turns into a cancerous wound and leads on to illness and depression, or creates violence and destruction. In counselling, before someone can move from apathy to exhilaration, they have to move through a state in which they get in touch with their anger – and express it.

This card is also saying that we should use our mouths a bit more in life by telling the other person what we want, what we are not prepared to put up with and when we are unhappy with them. We must learn to exercise this powerful device called our mouth! It really can have incredible effects once activated! You only have to remember a time when you got something off your chest by telling someone what you were really thinking to realise how powerful this experience can be.

Above all, the Tower acts as a karmic cleansing. The Tower not only affects people or situations, it also affects countries. Climate, floods, earthquake, wars, famine, tornadoes, volcanic eruptions are all tied up with the Tower. Certain countries or populations must go through a karmic cleansing in order to rise again.

Negative aspects of the Tower

vandalism	turmoil	tempestuous
crumbling down	mistake	ruin
fall	building castles in the air	harsh
'I know everything attitude'	fury/violence	rage/savage
destructive	misogyny	danger
	collapse	shape changer

Key words of the Tower

sudden	speed of light	fire
tension	agitation	impetuous
striking	warning/test	

Suggestions of the Tower

Be prepared when problems arise.
Don't suppress your anger, don't fear it. Direct it.
Use your energy constructively to initiate transformation and to disintegrate the old ways.

Be willing to change your old ways.
Don't turn your energy inward.
Build your life on stronger foundations.

17

The Star

The Water Bearer

> *Faith is an oasis in the heart which will never be reached by the caravan of thinking.*
>
> ANCIENT ISLAMIC PROVERB

You are out walking under a starry sky. The air is warm and gentle around you. The dome of heaven all about you is filled with its glorious gems, the stars and the Milky Way behind it. You stand there in amazement, poised between earth and air. You seem to grow in stature, becoming taller, until you can almost reach out and touch the stars themselves. Looking up to the Milky Way, you raise your arms and breathe deeply from its downpouring radiance. To your side you see a naked maiden. You cannot tell if she is human or angelic, but there is something about her which is almost fairy-like. Like the angel who you met earlier, she also holds water vessels, one in each hand. You speak out to her. What is her answer? How will you continue this scenario?

The Star card portrays a beautiful woman (the Goddess Nuit) pouring water from an urn to quench the thirst of humanity. This is the water of life that gives knowledge to all and knowledge gives life in return. Thus, the Star shows us how to nourish and water all that exists within and around so that it shall bear fruit. It is the never-ending flow of higher knowledge waiting for us to rise up on the staff of evolution, so as to be able to receive from it.

The Star is hinting that we all come from the same constellation, (the) Heaven(s). Each of us is a star. Unfortunately being on earth has separated us from each other. We have each developed differently. All misunderstandings and conflicts between human beings come from that separation of consciousness. Thus, the Star represents us as human beings getting together again and sharing thoughts and knowledge to help one another. The Star touches upon the principle of humanitarianism in life. This is the challenge of the New Age into which we are currently entering – can we set aside all the tribalism of the last ten thousand years and relate to each other in a new way?

The human race has shown itself to be extremely knowledgeable and inventive, but much of this knowledge is on the surface. We have still to confront the issues of overpopulation, pollution, war, famine, disease and suppression. What is the use of any knowledge if it is not oriented towards creating a better world? After all, we share this planet together.

When we talk about 'the Star', we need to ask, 'which Star?' There are various answers, but the main one is the Pole Star, which is taken by navigators as the most fixed point in the night sky and it is from this that they are able to plot their course. The real question is 'What is your Fixed Point', i.e. your point of reference. We all have certain 'landmarks' in our reality and things become very confusing when they start getting moved about. To a certain extent, we are all resistant to change and it is well known that one of the periods of greatest stress in our lives is when we have to move house. The other big one, of course, is dealing with bereavement. When everything is going fine in life, we are happy to coast along and not have to give too much thought to the central principles which make up our 'landmarks'. But when we have problems, unless we have a spiritual side, we will feel as helpless as a small ship floundering around in a storm. Having a spiritual side doesn't necessarily take away the storm. With it we can at least see the Pole Star from which we can get a better idea of where we are and how long it will take us to get beyond our present problems. The Pole Star is at the centre of our mystical universe. Around it hangs the Constellation Draconis and beyond this, the twelve signs of the Zodiac, against which the planets of our Solar System move.

In some versions of this Tarot card, it is not the Pole Star that is so emphasised. We see a single star, with six others in the background. What is being shown here is the Constellation Pleiades, or the Seven Sisters. They were the daughters of Atlas and Pleione. There are several versions of their lives, but the central theme is that although they were once mortal, they were changed into stars by Zeus and placed in the sky, alongside the Constellation Taurus. What we are seeing here is how we can receive help from divine sources.

The Star is the calm sea after the storm, as it represents tranquillity, serenity and peace of mind.

Negative aspects of the Star

racism	wastage/pollution	experimentation on animals
dictatorship	impersonality	following like sheep
disconnection	lack of concern for humanitarian issues	nuclear bombs and waste
suppression	wasting time on endless discussion	having faith in drugs and politicians

Key words of the Star

dreams come true/hopes	anchor	conquest of different spaces
telecommunications	aircraft	new waves
community	innovators	other forms of life
inventors	new possibilities	superior forces
communion	synthesis	links/unity
ideals		humanitarian

Suggestions of the Star

Learn about organic farming.

Learn to recycle, cut the wastage.

Be receptive to new changes or trends.

Think what you want to think.

Restore peace and love in your daily life.

See the universe out there, be part of it – better still, be a star!

Support humanitarian organisations/be concerned with worldwide issues.

Use your knowledge to create good for everyone.

18

The Moon

The Realm of the Subconscious

Every belief system is a different finger pointing to the moon.

ANCIENT HINDU MYSTIC

> *It is night, a faint sound of running water invites you to find out where it is coming from. You wander among trees of different kinds, over slopes of earth, past protruding rock formations. As you continue, the sound of water becomes increasingly louder. You turn a corner and see a waterfall, with a great oak tree standing beside it. You kneel down to drink from the little stream that runs from this cascade and as you do so you hear the sound of distant thunder. The oak leaves rustle as if in recognition of the sound. As you look into the sky, you see a glorious full moon shining. Something in you now feels complete. Continue your adventure and invent/discover the characters you would like to meet in this realm.*

The Moon represents the subconscious, the realm of dreams, fears, memories, every kind of thinking not connected with the here and now. It contains the hopes and fears of the future and all the recollections of things that have already taken place. Psychologists call the subconscious the shadow side because it contains hidden feelings and emotions which seem to irrationally influence our behaviour.

This part of the mind has fascinated psychologists and psychiatrists for hundred of years. In the States, psychiatry is big business. People have been labelled according to their irrationalities: manic depressive, schizophrenic, neurotic, etc. The tragedy is when people start defining themselves – let alone others – with these horrific titles.

It is interesting to look inwards and see what aspects of ourselves are different, eccentric, unpredictable, unreasonable. In any case, where is it written that we should be perfectly reasonable and predictable? I can't think of anything more boring!

The Moon also represents fear of the unknown. It can be a bit daunting to look inside your subconscious mind. It is very difficult to get to it, because we have built shields around it to protect it. It is in the back of our mind.

The Moon gives us a distorted reality, things are not quite as they seem or look. Think about it. If you walk under the moonlight, you can easily imagine all sort of spooky things around you. Suddenly there is a strange noise, someone is hiding behind a tree, a tree is after you, etc. This is the work of the imagination. Everything is blown out of proportion. A shadow of a squirrel could easily look like a dragon! And it is exactly what we experience when we are under the influence of the Moon. We are motivated by our imagination. Soap operas are the best example of the Moon's influence, as everything is overly dramatised all the time. This is what I call living life in the full Moon or in the twilight zone.

Many people have asked me how they might be able to develop their intuitive side. One answer to this is 'in silence'. You might have to go off for a period of time and just sit quietly, getting more and more in touch with your own 'inner voice'. There are monasteries, retreats, ashrams, etc. where you can do this, but the best way is the most direct, by going off for a long stroll by yourself right now. Doing is better than thinking about doing. The whole purpose behind meditation, prayer, etc. is stilling all the internal and external noises, so that we can get to the point of being more 'in tune' with the voice of the higher self. Then we can begin to receive divine guidance. We must listen to the voice of our conscience. This is the first stage in 'hearing' the 'Voice'.

> *Go off into the countryside with a backpack laden with food, water and a sleeping bag. Stay away for at least two days and two nights. Speak to no one. Write down all of your thoughts as you go along. Ask God/dess, your Holy Guardian Angel, guiding spirit, etc., to speak to you. See what happens!*

The Moon seems so gentle, sitting there in the sky. Yet it is extremely powerful, dragging millions of tons of water around the globe non-stop. So although it is a seemingly gentle influence, it is remarkably powerful. Underestimate it at your peril!

The Moon also symbolises reflection. It casts back the rays of the Sun, imparting them with its own internal qualities. Here in this card we are also able to take a look at how we reflect back to other people; at how in other people we see reflections of ourselves. Especially in our own children, we see our own face and then the face of the other parent. In those people around us, we see aspects of ourselves.

The things that we suspect others of are almost invariably things that we have done ourselves. The Moon is like a mirror, showing us a reflection of ourselves. It may not always be a pleasant picture. To look in that mirror may show us aspects of ourselves that we would rather not confront. Honesty is needed to shatter the illusions which we like to build up about ourselves.

The Moon also shows us about cycles, as it is the fastest moving astrological influence, moving through the Zodiac once a month. Many people start things off, but never get to the point of finishing them. They start by having a dream, or a picture of what they would like to accomplish, but somehow it never comes off.

Negative aspects of the Moon

touchy/moody	psychosomatic illnesses	overly sensitive
immature	living in a dream land	self-abnegation
abuse	Jekyll and Hyde	love and hate conflict
lunacy	complaining	delirium
PMT/ME	drama	vulnerability
absorbing people's negativity		
madness	asylum	unstable
escapist	vague	impressionable
weak-willed	sentimental	delirium
aberration	distress	afraid of darkness
subliminal	fears of deep water	affected
kisses under the moonlight		

Key words of the Moon

sacrifices	triggering	emanations
mothering		

| link | rehabilitation | instigating responses |
| acting | sensitivity | nurturing |

Suggestions of the Moon

Try to be aware of your reactions and feelings.

Look at your dreams, keep a dream diary.

Take time to listen to your inner self.

Keep your feet firmly on the ground, don't be so strongly
influenced by your emotions and imagination.

Learn to recognise and deal with your own feelings and emotions.

Remember that most of your fears will never happen.

Accept the way you are.

19

The Sun

The Godhead

*Let there be light – the light is within you – let
the light shine!*

MASONIC INVOCATION

*You find yourself in a beautiful garden, full of
flowers of every description, colour and scent.
Your senses are overwhelmed by the sight and
smell. You walk further into the garden and at
its centre you discover a fountain, from which
emerges a small rainbow cascade of water. You
drink from the cool water, noticing how cool it
is in your hands and in your mouth and throat.*

> *From behind you, you hear the sound of*
> *children's voices. As you turn around you see*
> *two children, both young, one boy and the other*
> *a girl. They could well be twins. They take you by*
> *the hand and lead you further into the garden.*
> *What happens to you this day?*

The Sun represents heat, light and life. Without light, we will be in a state of permanent darkness. Without heat, the air would be in a state of ice. This planet would in fact be a very desolate and abandoned place. Without the vibrant and exuberant presence of the Sun nothing could grow and develop. Now you start to understand why it is so important to turn to the Sun. For the Sun himself is our only guide. He illuminates our lives. If you know how to work with the Sun, the Sun will give us light (enlightenment), heat (warmth and love) and life (willpower to manifest). The Sun is the first creation made by God: 'Let there be light'.

When the Sun is out there in the sky, most people are working, doing, creating, on a physical, material level. Most of our work is done in daylight. We can see more clearly the reality of whatever we are dealing with. The Sun card is about objective truths, not just personal ones. **It is about action, construction, planning.** Before embarking on any major project, it is vital to construct a model of its workability before hand. We can't afford to just rush into anything on the basis that 'my intuition told me so'. If intuition is grounded in any kind of reality, then it won't do any harm at all to see if the objective conditions support that.

The Sun card touches upon the kind of work we do, as individuals, as well as emphasising the importance of work in itself. Without work, people become dispirited, depressed, listless. Morale is directly related to productivity. The more productive a person feels, the higher will be their level of morale.

This card is asking us how we could each go about making the kinds of changes to our work lives that we would like to see taking place.

In the future, when all our natural resources are fully exhausted, the Sun will be the major source of energy. In fact, we can find everything we need in the Sun. The rays of the Sun carry vitamin D which brings us great vitality and strength. The Sun is a subtle energy, in that a little goes a long way.

In Yoga, one of the most important exercises is called Salute to the Sun and is an excellent way of stretching the body first thing in the morning.

The Sun radiates the colours of the rainbow and thus enhances the colours all around us. On a sunny day, the sky is bright blue, the leaves bright green, etc. Thus, the Sun is showing how we can use the same colours and qualities to reinforce our aura. We can radiate the colours of the Sun. Imagine yourself every day bathing in purple, blue, green, yellow, orange and red light. Work with colours more. Study them. If you want to see the colours in the rays of the Sun, use a prism.

The Sun card teaches us about physical exercise. The Greek Olympics were dedicated to Apollo, the god of the Sun. At the beginning of the Games, even to this day, we still have the ceremony of lighting the flame, which is another symbol of Apollo and represents the fire being brought down from the sun to humanity.

This card is asking us what we are doing to take care of our bodies. Everybody – at every age – has the need to do some kind of sport or exercise. Also, what are we doing to get the effects of pollution out of our systems?

One of the most important energy centres is the Solar Plexus; Solar, of course, pertaining to the Sun. It is from the Solar Plexus that we find our centre, the basis of our power.

The next time the Sun is shining, go out into your garden, or a park, and remove any clothes which cover your stomach area. As you lay down, centre your attention on this area of your body and breathe deeply, bringing the air deep down into the bottom of your lungs. Letting your breath rise and fall, imagine a tiny flower bud opening up around your navel region. Allow it to absorb the beneficial energies that the warm Sun is giving it. Let it begin to grow and blossom. Let yourself 'see' its colours and smell its fragrance. Enjoy this space for a few minutes. When you are ready, make a note of how you are feeling and open your eyes slowly.

Negative aspects of the Sun

sunburn	burning one's fingers	over-extension
over-doing	desert	things drying out
skin cancer	sunbeds	major holiday resorts next to beaches
blindness	waste of energy	

Key words of the Sun

open-hearted	authentic	beauty
happiness	creative	luminous
alive	penetration	celebration

79

harmonious   radiating   vacation
ultimate love

Suggestions of the Sun

Do not abuse the sun. The Sun's rays are beneficial in small doses, dangerous in larger doses.

Acknowledge his presence every day and thank him.

Learn to use the Sun's energy.

Only the luminous path of wisdom leads to truth.

Learn to be like the Sun. Love like the Sun.

Go for a walk in the park or the countryside if you want to know the Sun.

May your thoughts be as luminous as the Sun.

Grow and develop with the Sun.

20

Judgement

The Last Exit

Without transformation, progress is not possible.

ANON

> *You find yourself walking through a desert scene. There is no sound or movement here. The heat is unbearable. You look up to the sky and see the dazzling sun in its canopy of blue. You continue walking through the desert, the sand starts running into the sides of your boots. As you move forward, you can actually feel your body*

> *dehydrating. You start having hallucinations about water – imagining rivers, streams, waves. You continue further and feel the ground trembling beneath your feet. As you look, cracks open in the earth's surface and the ground starts gaping open. What happens now? Continue this scenario.*

Judgement is about major changes, or transformation taking place in our lives. The title Judgement could suggest a Biblical 'Day of Judgement', where all souls would be judged by a strict deity. The actual meaning is more concerned with how we might well be judging others and even ourselves. When we are finally able to stop that, then we shall truly experience a powerful transformation in our lives.

This card is asking us to look at the major changes which our own lives have seen: can we see how we have changed as people through them? Have we mellowed and become better people, or worse?

Major changes can be very painful. **We all have to go through pain to experience release from it.** Do we ever think of what a caterpillar goes through before it becomes a butterfly? What about those athletes competing professionally? Do we ever think of all the pain and suffering they had to go through in order to reach the top? For them it's not pain – it's the thought of fulfillment at the end that keeps them going.

This card has an association with pressure and asks us how we each respond to this. How do we respond to pain? It is an interesting exercise to sit down and write about our own experiences in this regard, making the accounts highly descriptive and detailed.

81

This card is also about how we can change instead of skimming along the surface of problems and simply coping. So many people are reacting with their problems, illnesses, boyfriends, work, etc. instead of making the kinds of changes that *really* need to take place. We must learn to take action, because by simply coping we are not doing any favours for anyone.

Negative aspects of Judgement

manipulative	cannot be stopped	imposing
guilt/shame	phobias	obsessions
fanatic	elimination	too much pressure

Key words of Judgement

turning point	overcoming obstacles	emigration
resurrection	urges/cataclysm	assimilation
intense	self-discovery	awakening
by-passing	alteration	analysis
reform	upheaval	motivation
pressure		transformative

Suggestions of Judgement

Be more adaptable.

Don't judge others or yourself.

Explore yourself.

Change instead of coping.

Try hypnotherapy or self-hypnosis to get rid of your problems.

21

The World

The Universe

> *Life is but an act and the world a stage.*
>
> W. SHAKESPEARE

> *Before you stands a woman, naked, except for a single length of purple silk which is draped across her shoulders. She dances before you and in her dancing you see something incredibly symbolic of your own life and of your Journey up to this point. But as you continue looking, you see another symbol, that of the dance of the earth around the sun and the beginning and end of all things. Everything seems to be contained in the movements of this dancing girl. You find yourself mesmerised. She invites you to join her in this dance, she beckons you to get up out of your seat in the audience and become her dancing partner. Join her!*

The World is the last card of the major Arcana and the fulfilment of each of them, if their lessons have been properly applied. The world represents success through your hard work. Not just in a materialistic sense either, but more in the sense of having conquered all the barriers which have led up to this point.

The World is about commitments and how we fulfil them: obligations to ourselves, our family, our environment, humanity in general.

This card is asking us if we have fulfilled our commitments and if not, what are we going to do about them?

The World represents trust too. Trust is the firmest foundation in human relationships, and without it nothing can be achieved. Trustworthiness is a highly esteemed commodity. When one has it, one is considered valuable. When one has lost it, one may be considered worthless. The World demonstrates how one can earn trust.

Can you be trusted? Do you keep your word? If you don't trust others, recall a time when you yourself were unworthy of trust.

The World card teaches us about limitations and responsibilities and therefore calls our attention towards those things in our lives that limit us, or to which we have duties. People rapidly lose their sense of self-value when they don't keep promises. Children completely lose respect for their parents when they find that they don't keep their promises to them. People lose respect for politicians who go back on their electoral promises. The teaching of loyalty to one's friends and fulfilling one's duties is an important one which a lot of people may have especial trouble in learning. Although the emphasis these days is on personal freedom, this card is here to remind us that without respect for the rights of others, there can be no personal freedom in the long run. We must respect our neighbour's space and if that means turning down the radio if it is troubling them, then that is what we must do. We can live our life as we wish, without forcing other people to share in it if they don't want to. Thus, the World card teaches us lessons of self-restraint.

This card is about law and people abiding by agreed processes. It is about people being able to place trust in the hands of those who are going to act with responsibility on behalf of them. When this breaks down – as it can – society begins to dissolve into anarchy.

This card rules over the seasons and the preparatory work that needs to be done to secure a harvest. It shows us that in order to reap, we must first of all sow and then carefully tend and look after that which we have sown. I once worked on a farm and I can certainly say that it was spiritually one of the most illuminating experiences of my life. It certainly gets you in touch with so many of this card's great teachings. Its teachings have nothing to do with books, with clever-clever debates, or pretty arguments, but with realities.

Excessive World card qualities result in people feeling that they must live their lives according to somebody else's expectations. They end up unhappy, yet too afraid to make a change. They end up feeling that they are carrying the World on their shoulders.

Do you feel you have too many responsibilities or obligations? How can you be discharged from them?

Negative aspects of the World

martyrdom	lack of confidence	carrying the world
heavy burdens		on one's shoulders
can't grasp money	can't fulfil	
or material issues		commitments

Key words of the World

labour	duty	up-holding
track record	wise	worldly success
reliable	pomegranates	finality

achieving	realising	manifesting
reality	recognition	handling situations

Suggestions of the World
Be responsible for yourself and others and the planet.
Help people who have helped you.
Don't carry unnecessary burdens.
Act with confidence.
Look at what you have achieved so far.
Be thankful and grateful for your success.

THE MINOR ARCANA

The minor arcana shows us 56 different everyday life situations, including 16 court cards which describe personality-types, or 'archetypes' – different kinds of people and influences that make up our lives. This section of the Tarot gives us a great deal of guidance to how we can be more effective and empower ourselves so that we can in turn empower others.

The Suit of Coins, Pentacles or Disks

This suit represents the element Earth. It stands for material and financial conditions. In ordinary playing cards, it is shown as the suit of Diamonds.

Ace of Coins

The Ace of Coins represents the purest form of the element of earth. It symbolises the gold or the precious stones that have taken millions of years to appear from the bowels of the earth. Thus, this card represents opportunities that spring up from the physical universe. It deals with reality and practicality.

This card transforms your skills or talents into **assets**. It is the doorway for the creative powers of the spirit. It is through this card that we can benefit financially or materially from what we know and can do.

It also teaches us essential spiritual lessons such as: to be of good temper, hard working, patient, resolute and caring.

The Ace of Coins is, therefore, a great channel for nourishment and sustenance.

Key words
lucrative business
beneficial
fruitful
profitable
worthwhile
revenue
gains
earning
anchor point
satisfaction
resources
stability

root
foundation
contracts

Negative aspects
out of touch with the physical universe

Two of Coins

The Two of Coins represents movement from one financial or material condition to the next.

The earth element is characterised by its immobility. That is why this card represents versatility in the physical universe. We need to become more adaptable or flexible in what we do. That way, we can easily develop different skills, or relocate and work somewhere else without any trouble or difficulty.

Key words
different circumstances or places
continuity
transition
juggling with work and personal life
part-time work
change

Negative aspects
fixity
rigidity
dislike of change
stuck in a rut

Three of Coins

The Three of Coins represents learning new skills or abilities. It is on earth that we learn to skilfully master matter, and to develop talents or gifts for this lifetime.

This card encourages us to learn practical and useful skills to get on with life. It could be on the work side or in other areas of life. A person is only useful when of help to the community.

Many years ago, people knew how to build houses, or make clothing, or how to hunt in order to survive. What do we have left from them? That is why this card urges us to regain those fundamental life skills.

What would you like to learn?

Key words
self-sufficiency
never too late
learning the basics
being practical

Negative aspects
relying on others to do it all
not interested in learning

Four of Coins

The Four of Coins represents power on the material level. This card is much concerned with one's own security – financial or material.

When we have a regular source of income, or we have saved some money, we feel more comfortable, we can relax and enjoy life, because we don't have to worry all the time about how we going to pay the bills. What we have accumulated will be sufficient for us to feel safe. It reminds us of the pyramid representing human needs. We have to feel secure on the material level before we can feel secure on other levels.

This card encourages us to make use of our financial or material gains.

The four gives us firmness and stability.

How can you make yourself more secure?

Key words
consolidation
fortress
reserved
conservative
saving
accumulation
possession
calculation
protection

Negative aspects
physical or material self-gratification
greed
hiding behind a wall of money
avarice
resources lying dormant

Five of Coins

The Five of Coins represents unexpected or unforeseen financial or material loss. In order to manifest gains or rewards on the physical level, we must first conquer the element of earth. It means that if one hasn't developed any skills or abilities to get on with life, one will have great difficulty in finding a job, or earning a living.

Also, in this card, there is a feeling of neediness. We need to be needed. People have to look after us all the time. We must change this equation in order to progress. Look after you.

Thus, this card encourages us to confront our inabilities in order to transcend them. We needs to develop skills or abilities, to stop being so needed by others and to plan ahead.

Key words
necessity
weakness
social limitation

Negative aspects
poverty
looking for sympathy
putting the blame on others or circumstances
lack of self worth
looking for someone to nurse
accidental expenses

Six of Coins

The Six of Coins represents the law of commerce, thus exchanges. We need to trade or sell or work in order to gain something back. That is the law of trade. This card is much concerned with ownership and self-evaluation of one's abilities or skills.

If we give our time or our skills, we must expect something in return. Otherwise, things are out of balance. We can be as generous as we want to, as long as we know how to discriminate. Where do you draw the line when you give or exchange?

The lesson of the Six of Coins is to work in a mutual exchange with people. Don't disadvantage yourself just to please others. Value your work, or a skill you have, and ask for something in return.

Key words
trade
industry
balancing
accounting
business strategy
transaction
forecasting
speculation

Negative aspects
spending more than you are earning
wasting time and effort
giving to the undeserving

Seven of Coins

The Seven of Coins represents the harvest time springing up from the fruits of our labour. If we make an effort, and we are willing to work hard, we shall reap the rewards of our work. We can only reap what we have sown.

Here we have the principle of cultivating one's skills and abilities. In this card, we are mainly governed by the seasons, so we have to wait for the right season to harvest what we have sown. A tree doesn't grow overnight. Be patient and persevere.

Thus, this card encourages us to keep ourselves busy. If we are busy, we are productive, therefore we can be appreciative and ready when the harvest comes. What do you cultivate in your life?

Key words
reliable
manifestation
realisation
growth
patience
perseverance

Negative aspects
workaholic
harvesting somebody else's hard work
laziness
expecting miracles

Eight of Coins

The Eight of Coins represents craftsmanship. Craftsmanship is simply the mastery of one's skills through self-discipline and determination.

In order to be good at what we want to do, we must practise again and again. Practice makes perfect. It reminds me of dancers, who must work at their craft all the time, day in and day out. They are truly dedicated. That is why at the end of the day, the craftsman enjoys his work because he turned a pleasure into his work and his work into a pleasure.

Key words
apprentice
in demand
specialisation
order
careful
manual skills
the arts
meticulous

Negative aspects
too perfectionist
too demanding on oneself
not practising

Nine of Coins

The Nine of Coins represents recognition in the eyes of others. In this card, we have been acknowledged for our work. We feel satisfied because we have gained material status and esteem from our peers. We are appreciated. We value our work, and our work is valued.

Thus, this card represents achievement on the material level. Have people ever noticed your work and effort?

Key words
fame
promotion
rank
prize
success
increase

Negative aspects
showing off
ego in the way of doing
peacock
put on pedestal
obsessed with appearance

Ten of Coins

The Ten of Coins represents joint financial decisions or major investments.

In many ways, this card shows the importance of 'family' or communal business. We must preserve our inheritance, and participate with other people to build a new house, city, country, etc.

Thus, this card represents us sharing what we know with other people in order to profit together. Do you work for yourself or with others?

Key words
corporation
financial commitment
deals
employers

Negative aspects
profit not shared
big income for bosses but dangerous conditions and low pay
for workers
not viable

Page of Coins

The Page of Coins represents someone who is looking for a new direction in life or new responsibilities.

This card looks at one's pursuits in life. What do you want to achieve at the end of the day? Would you like to be in the same situation for years or would you like to have more control over your life?

That is why we must look ahead in order to plan for the future. What do we want to have or be?

Key words
first job
doing something completely different
new horizons
improvement

Negative aspects
lack of concern
no control over one's profession
missing opportunities to progress

Knight of Coins

The Knight of Coins represents a man who is keen to develop the
work aspect of his life. That is why this man wants to develop his
skills and abilities in order to progress. He has something to look
forward to in life and work. Do you have objectives too?

Key words of the Knight
organise
well-prepared
persistent
ambition
planning
professional
projects

Negative aspects of the Knight
lost his sense of direction
unemployed
bored with work/can't find his vocation

Queen of Coins

The Queen of Coins represents a woman who is keen to develop the
work side of her life. She wants to be involved in the financial or
material aspects. She likes the good things in life.

97

She represents the nurturing aspect of any creative process – the intermediary steps by which an idea is turned into a reality. Care, precision and frugality are her hallmarks. Under her influence, 'customer satisfaction' and a high level of service are guaranteed.

Key words of the Queen
independent financially
appreciative of good things in life
practical with money
knows how to budget

Negative aspects of the Queen
lost her sense of direction
confused
bored with life

King of Coins

The King of Coins represents someone at the top of whatever they are doing. In this card, we see achievement through one's own effort and talents. This person has mastered the physical universe, and is also very encouraging and supportive towards others.

When we look at successful people, it seems as though their good fortune has come easily. What we don't see are the dedication, hard times, sacrificed love life and family life that have gone into the melting pot of their good fortune.

This card encourages us to flourish and prosper. It is possible.

Key words of the King
steady
permanent
prodigal
loans
calculated
administrative

Negative aspects of the King
dull
working with figures
talks business all the time

The Suit of Cups

This suit is linked with the element of water. It represents the subjective world of inner experiences, such as feelings, emotions and sensations. In ordinary playing cards, it is shown as the suit of Hearts.

Ace of Cups

The Ace of Cups represents the purest form of the element of water. Water is the symbol of matter on which the spirit works to give it form, for the principal property of water is its adaptability. Its second characteristic is that it can be impregnated.

In this card, we have the mere representation of the highest qualities of love and of joy; its spring which wells up within us. We feel flooded with gratitude towards all the beauty which surrounds us. Our souls overflow with love. Our feelings are as pure as the water from mountain springs! Love has finally ripened.

99

Key words

contentment

birth

abundance

translucency

conducting

happiness

joy

vivified

kindness

peace

fullness

Negative aspects

on an artificial high

not fully happy

emptiness

impurity

Two of Cups

The Two of Cups represents a new relationship, or a new stage (beginning) within an existing relationship. In this card, we have the mutual exchange of feelings and emotions. We are willing to share our experiences and should be open to new friendships or relationships. How close are your relationships?

Key words

new friendships

love

contacts

harmony

renewal
affinity

Negative aspects
locked in a relationship
can't receive from others
don't want to know

Three of Cups

The Three of Cups represents reunion or getting together with old friends or relatives. This card shows how we can reciprocate feelings of love or friendship to each other. Beauty is all around. There is a feeling of celebration, of joyfulness. We feel loved, therefore we love in return. Love is healing. Are you loved by somebody else?

Key words
eating
drinking
marriage
meeting old friends

Negative aspects
can't feel love
avoiding old friends
not enjoying people's company

Four of Cups

The Four of Cups represents reaching out for new friendships or relationships.

This card usually talks about things we take for granted. We are looking for someone or something, and when it finally comes into our life, we just can't be bothered. There is always an excuse or something holding us back for not socialising, or going out, or accepting an invitation, etc. What is stopping you from reaching out?

Key words
taking what is on offer
making the first move
opportunities to meet people
reaching out

Negative aspects
holding back
waiting for things to happen without effort
withdrawal

Five of Cups

The Five of Cups represents dependency on others. In this card, we tend to cling too much to people's promises or words. It also shows disappointment which results from the failure of reality to match expectations.

We are like little babies waiting for our mother to change us, because we can't do it on our own. And when she doesn't come back, we feel completely lost. When people don't follow through their commitments, we feel let down or betrayed. People are not perfect, they often talk about or promise more than they can deliver, but it doesn't really mean that they do not care for you either. That is why this card encourages us to look ahead, instead of depending on or lamenting those broken promises.

Key words
relying too heavily on other people
caring
be more rational

Negative aspects
disillusionment
disappointment
sadness
living in the past

Six of Cups

The Six of Cups represents learning to give and receive emotionally. When it comes to affection or love, we have to give in order to receive, and to receive in order to give.

This card shows us how we can develop our relationships into a long-lasting friendship or love affair. With the Six of Cups, we are full of good intentions for each other. We feel like children again. There is a sense of harmony. Are you able to get in touch with your 'child within'?

Key words
friendship
affinity
socialising
growing relationship
gifts

Negative aspects
giving without receiving and vice versa
expecting something in return

Seven of Cups

The Seven of Cups represents emotional confusion. What are your priorities in life? You might want to be rich, or be a farmer, or have many boyfriends, or look like Marilyn Monroe. Whatever you want to be, you have to sort out what comes first in your life.

Life is not like Hollywood. We must come down from our comforting clouds every now in order to realise our desires. What do you want in life? What seems to be important for you?

Key words
being realistic
using dreams constructively

Negative aspects
daydreams
fantasies
escapism
make-believe

Eight of Cups

The Eight of Cups represents our quest for a deeper meaning in life. Where is our life taking us? We must each find our own individual destiny. What is life all about? What is the purpose of it? What do we have to realise?

This card shows us the way. The answer is within us. We come here to acquire what we lack. But very few realise what they really need.

What is life offering you now? Have you found any answers?

Key words
reflection
understanding
pondering
depth
searching

Negative aspects
looking for a substitute
denying deep emotional needs
puzzle
superficiality

Nine of Cups

The Nine of Cups represents experiencing life as a celebration. We must enjoy life and celebrate it. Learn to feel happiness flowing through you. Surely, life is not that bad. Are you thanking life?

Let's not forget that no matter how bad things are – or have been – we are still better off than many people on this planet. Let's be grateful for our eyesight, for the fact that we can walk, or hear. We must learn to look on the bright side.

To celebrate, we don't need to drink or get 'out of it'. Alcohol and drugs more often just bring us down. We must learn to enjoy life without these intoxicants/stimulants. Then we can enjoy life's 'natural high'.

Key words
parties
eating
drinking
good things in life
earthly pleasure

Negative aspects
being happy but only on the surface
too many parties
excessive eating or drinking

Ten of Cups

The Ten of Cups represents an emotional commitment. It shows a union or communion with others or oneself. We have a mission to accomplish.

We have to be committed in anything we feel or do in order to get involved in our life. When we commit ourselves, we feel at one with the universe. We only get out of any relationship what we put into it. Even then there isn't any exact mechanism of exchange. We might put in everything we have emotionally only to come out with nothing. On other occasions we might end up in a relationship with someone who is quite devoted but not enough for us. What do we do then? For some of us, this is the tough one.

This card represents personal integrity.

Key words
marriage
dedication
unity

Negative aspects
unstable
don't want to get involved

Page of Cups

The Page of Cups represents new social or professional contacts. We are so comfortable and safe at home, around people we know, that it is very difficult to fly away with our own wings. In order to grow emotionally, we must start to meet new people. And then we can learn about ourselves, and how to build new affinities. It is time for us to experience new feelings and emotions.

When we enter a room full of people, we automatically judge people and mentally cross them off our list of interesting men and women. We all do this, whether or not we are aware of it. This card is inviting us to go beyond this point and to give new people a chance to enter our lives.

Key words
learning about oneself through others
romance
'breaking the egg'

Negative aspects
too introverted
withdrawn
feeling insecure
shy
naive

Knight of Cups

The Knight of Cups represents sensitivity or receptivity in a man. In this card, a man is looking for a meaningful relationship. This is his Quest.

The Knight shows the active impulse. He brings out those feelings which involve taking the initiative. When we feel those emotional needs banging on the door of our mind, we should go with them. Who knows where they might lead us? If we ignore them, we will just remain bored and unfulfilled. By letting them guide us we might well have a lot of fun!

Key words of the Knight
flirty
dreamy
artistic

Negative aspects of the Knight
can't express himself emotionally
too impressionable
sentimental

Queen of Cups

The Queen of Cups represents sensitivity or receptivity in a woman. In this card, she looks quite contented. She represents the receptive side of our emotional nature, i.e. our individual ability to enjoy all the different emotions or feelings which are brought out by someone entering or staying in our lives.

Our minds often censor many feelings. Due to social conditioning, most men are uncomfortable with emotions which show gentleness, love, playfulness; all this is unmanly. In reality, only a man who is completely confident about his masculinity can enjoy getting in touch with his own Queen of Cups within himself.

When we can stop censoring our feelings, and let ourselves experience *all* the range of emotions which life brings out in us, then, and only then, we can be truly happy.

Key words of the Queen
artistic
caring
mother figure
stable

Negative aspects of the Queen
easily impressionable
insensitive to people's needs
taking for granted
sentimental

King of Cups

The King of Cups represents an emotional mature man. He is in a sense the charmer of the pack. He looks quite contented in everything he does. He knows how to give and receive.

He also represents a kind of emotional coming of age. This is when we no longer fixate on people with whom we have nothing in common. We have driven down enough dead ends to know when we are getting nowhere. This card indicates a sense of emotional maturity, for either a man or a woman. No longer do we need to get upset if someone we find attractive doesn't want to know. We now have the ability to move on without attachment.

Key words of the King
stable
eccentric
creative
father figure

Negative aspects of the King
dull
pleasing others
between two seas
too sugary

The Suit of Swords

This suit represents the element of Air. It symbolises states of mind, and states of conflict. In ordinary playing cards, it is shown as the suit of Spades.

Ace of Swords

The Ace of Swords represents the purest form of the element of air. Air represents the mental body (thoughts) and the nervous system. Air is rational, it is the objective world.

Thus, this card represents a breakthrough of some kind on the mental level. The sword represents our thoughts, the clouds represent our negative feelings. The Ace of Swords distinguishes, separates and arranges, so as to clarify where we stand.

Key words

determination

Excalibur

intelligence

rapidity

clear-headed

penetration

wind

victory

Negative aspects

self-limiting thoughts

inability to think clearly

difficulty in communication

over-analytical

can't concentrate

Two of Swords

The Two of Swords represents indecision. What should we do? Which way should we go? Here we have the conflict between mind (thought) and heart (feeling).

The mind alone cannot see very far, it needs the helping hand of the heart in order to understand better where we stand. This card shows us how we can balance both mind and heart.

Are your mind and heart in conflict when it comes to making a decision?

Key words
see both sides
balance
crossroads
turning point

Negative aspects
ignoring feelings
don't want to see

Three of Swords

The Three of Swords represents heartbreak unless one can communicate better.

Here we have been hurt deep inside. Instead of talking it through with the person(s) concerned we have decided, on the subconscious level, to remain silent and to suffer for it. It is almost like a self-inflicted pain. At this stage, our grey feelings have overcast our rational thoughts.

We must communicate what is in our heart before the pain we feel is turned into grief and resentment. What is stopping you talking about your pain? If the other person in your emotional crisis doesn't want to talk with you, find someone – a friend, counsellor, whatever – who will. Communication is the hundred per cent effective remedy for a broken heart.

It is so difficult for each of us to truly open up in this way. But only when we get it all off our chest – the hurt, rejection, humiliation and loss – can we start afresh.

With this card, it feels like it has only ever happened to you, but believe me, we all have this experience in common.

Key words
personal
using words to express pain

Negative aspects
hiding to cry
pain in the heart
upset

Four of Swords

The Four of Swords represents worries and tensions. Here we have to relax more in order to let go of all negative thoughts.

This card teaches us to be alert, lucid and aware of what's going on inside us. We must be selective in what we are thinking. Are you a worrier, and if so what can you do to stop it?

Take time to go for walks in the park in order to empty your mind. Take some time off to relax. Learn to breathe properly; breathing helps to slow down the brain waves.

Key words
release
calm
slow down

Negative aspects
stress
tired
anxious

Five of Swords

The Five of Swords represents the parting of ways. Here we have the end of a battle, we feel defeated.

This card encourages us to be careful of unnecessary quarrels. The loss will be ours. Do you start to quarrel when you know you have nothing to fall back on?

Key words
troublesome
retreat
casualties

Negative aspects
separation
pessimistic
rejection
lies
deceit
tears
shame

Six of Swords

The Six of Swords represents moving away from negativity. Difficulties are overcome by finding new ideas. Here we are looking for solutions to our problems. Ask yourself how you could possibly change your situation. Soon you will find the answers. When you are in a rut, do you look for solutions?

In particular this card shows withdrawal – retreat. Sometimes we have to pull out of a situation in order to deal with it. To others this may seem like running away. But many battles have been won by an army retreating, getting itself reorganised and then dealing with the opposing force. There is no shame in pulling out, if that is what seems best for us at the time.

Key words
thinking through
spontaneous thinking
brainstorming
suggestion

Negative aspects
static thinking
not searching

Seven of Swords

The Seven of Swords represents sacrifices. One has to give up something good for something better in order to progress in life.

Having to make a sacrifice every now and then is part of our daily life. We must not be stopped by our self-limiting thoughts all the time. We must look beyond them. Leave your excess thoughts behind and see how light you can become.

Another aspect of this card is being 'ripped off'. In the picture, we can see something being carried away surreptitiously. To protect what is ours we do have to exercise vigilance – not to the point of being paranoid and thinking like a security guard, but just a background awareness of what is going on and of the possible consequences of being too open. There is a lot of bad out there.

Key words
progress
stealth
sorting out

Negative aspects
coward
ripping off
not willing to let go our self-limiting thoughts

Eight of Swords

The Eight of Swords represents frustration. Here we can learn to be a bit more patient.

This card epitomises restrictions we are imposing willingly or unwillingly upon ourselves. Because we remain blindfolded, we are not really seeing what the real problems are, or where they are coming from. What are they?

Key words
can't escape
trapped
finding
waiting

Negative aspects
bondage
victim
impatient
stress
disconnection

Nine of Swords

The Nine of Swords represents isolation. Here we have to learn to open up new lines or channels of communication. We must talk about what is holding us back. It seems in this card that we must go through a confessional in order to set ourselves free from the prison we have created. What is holding you back?

This card is a little like the Three of Swords, only here we have a stronger sense of loneliness and isolation. In some decks we see a woman crying on a bed. I find this picture especially moving. Many of us are afraid to love for fear of this happening to us.

But if we are not prepared to risk the hell-state of this card, how can we possibly deserve the paradise-state of love when we do find it?

Key words
recognise
reveal
isolation
admit
truth

Negative aspects
guilt
hands are tied
things we have done wrong
depression
repression

Ten of Swords

In the Ten of Swords, we have to acknowledge the end of an era in order to begin another one. Here, we experience pain and/or suffering, and there is nothing we can do to stop it. We must accept it; we must be tolerant of our mistakes, or other people's mistakes. Instead of dwelling on loss and pain we must learn to forgive and let go. Major changes are coming, go along with them to turn them to your advantage. Can you forgive?

Key words
result
out of one's system

Negative aspects
poison running in blood
mental anguish
revenge
disgust

Page of Swords

The Page of Swords represents eagerness to rush into battles or conflicts. Here we have someone quite inexperienced in dealing with his own ego. This card encourages us not to rush into conclusion or fighting other people's fights. Because, at the end of the day, it is you who is going to get hurt!

Key words
willing to stand
insecure
not knowing all facts and figures

Negative aspects
don't start something you can't stop
unprotected

Knight of Swords

The Knight of Swords represents power by manipulation or force. When it refers to ourselves, we have to learn to be more tactful or diplomatic.

When this card shows someone else or another influence in our lives, it is a warning for us not to hand over our rights too easily. Often it can show force being threatened or brought to bear against us, with the implication of loss if we resist it.

Almost always this threat evaporates when challenged: it takes courage to resist, but this is the only way of overcoming the danger and protecting what is important to us.

Key words
balance of power
gentleness

Negative aspects
aggressive with words
impetuous
stroppy
invalidation
angry

Queen of Swords

The Queen of Swords represents a determined woman who has erected barriers between herself and others.

This woman is very difficult to approach, she stands strongly in her position. In this card, we are reminded that beautiful things sometimes have thorns. Be careful!

In some older versions of the tarot, it was said that this card showed a divorced woman. Just as the world has changed, so to has the tarot which reflects it. This card can show the kind of woman who knows what she wants, and isn't inhibited about going after it. If only there were more like her!

Key words
be open
maintaining your barriers
don't be negative
keeping your own space

Negative aspects
critical
revengeful
stubborn

cold
questioning
inquiring
suspicious

King of Swords

The King of Swords represents someone who has won the war, and now has to establish the peace.

This card reminds us of the Cold War. Here, we have someone of authority who is on guard all the time. We must learn to allow people to express themselves instead of judging them non-stop. You can establish your own authority by allowing others to occupy centre stage more. Allow your own role to be a more distant one, without being involved in all the petty crises and disputes. You will need intermediaries – people you can trust and to whom you can delegate your own power.

Key words
enjoying life
be open minded
allow mistakes

Negative aspects
military
intolerant
bitter
headstrong
prejudicial

The Suit of Wands

This suit represents the element of Fire. It symbolises energy, action and will-power. In ordinary playing cards it is shown as Clubs.

Ace of Wands

The Ace of Wands represents the purest form of the element of fire. Fire is the element of energy. It directs, orders and provides guidance.

Fire gives us inspiration, warmth and heat, love and light.

This card emphasises energy and action. It stands for new initiative or enterprise which has been activated. Individuality is brought forth and emphasised, not compromised.

Key words
action
will-power
vitality
truth
consume
creativity
dynamic

Negative aspects
lack of initiative
lack of energy

Two of Wands

The Two of Wands represents the giving and receiving of good advice. Now act upon it.

This card encourages us to exchange our ideas and to put them into motion. We need that outflow of energy to see if what we have to offer is workable. What do you think of this idea, shall we work it out together? We make the decision at the end of the day.

Are you a good advisor to yourself?

Key words
starting off new ideas
listening to people's point of view

Negative aspects
ask for help, but don't listen when it's given
wait for people to start off ideas
can't make decisions

Three of Wands

The Three of Wands represents leading the way by your own example. Here we have to initiate what we want to create. People will only be able to follow us if we take the first step. If we preach something that we are not doing, people will not follow us. If you tell a child not to smoke or take drugs because it is dangerous and you yourself are smoking like a chimney or drinking like a fish, do you think he is likely to listen to you? Hardly.

In this card, we find the principle of leadership. Are you a leader, i.e. do you show the way for others?

Key words
operative
purposeful
inspiration
honest
demonstrating
dominion

Negative aspects
talking but not doing
lack of will

Four of Wands

The Four of Wands represents participating with others toward a common goal. Here we have the principle of working together for the greater good of all.

In this card, we learn how to help and support each other. We learn about teamwork and co-operative work. We feel we have the same ideals or objectives. It emphasises being able to harmonise with others so that more than just our own personal objectives can be attained.

Key words
dynamics of life
completion
building a better world

Negative aspects
feel useless
can't belong

Five of Wands

The Five of Wands represents fierce competition. We need to push forward with determination in order to get our point or idea across.

This card represents challenges. We have to fight amicably of course, in order to sustain what we want to create. Are you competitive enough?

We each of us at times must fight hard for what we want. Evelyne and I went through a Five of Wands situation with the birth of our daughter Claudia. For Evelyne this card showed the pains and battles of birthing. For me it manifested in battling with the nurses in the hospital for proper attention for Evelyne and with the anaesthetists for sufficient medication. Although we had aimed for natural childbirth, when Claudia started on her way this was quickly shown to be quite impossible. This was a real Five of Wands test for all three of us!

Key words
argumentative
games
courage
sport
drive
strive

Negative aspects
friction
over imposing
too aggressive
hasty

Six of Wands

The Six of Wands represents victory. Here, we have accomplished our task. We feel admired by others, so we feel proud of ourselves. What have you accomplished?

Each of us has accomplished something – having a child, keeping down a job, showing bravery in the face of a mugging or a car accident. So we haven't all made piles of money or got ourselves to Hollywood. But there are many kinds of achievement, and who is to say which kind is superior to any other?

Key words
winning
achievement
confidence
self-esteem
be notice
impressive

Negative aspects
too vain
pomposity
pretence

Seven of Wands

The Seven of Wands represents having to tackle your problems one at a time before they overwhelm you.

Here we have to confront our problems or difficulties before we can achieve anything else. Do you confront or run away from your problems? Instead, why not write them down, in order of their magnitude. Now try and work out how you could navigate your way through them.

Imagine yourself as the protagonist in a novel or film, who has to fight to get out of a particularly nasty situation. Don't make it too easy (i.e. winning the lottery), but 'see' yourself actually resolving each issue one by one, in a practical way.

Key words
effort
courage
obstacles
handle

Negative aspects
overtaken
erratic
ignoring issues
overwhelming

Eight of Wands

The Eight of Wands represents the principle of life speeding up. Here we are very busy, there are lot of activities and much movement.

Things or ideas are taking off. We are travelling at the speed of light.

When we 'get on a roll', new ideas and projects open before us. The mother of all action is enthusiasm, so we have to stay positive. Looking forward to the future with eagerness doesn't imply being blind to the practical steps we must take to turn our projects into reality, but it does say we mentally can turn the 'problems' into 'opportunities'.

Key words
action
many ideas
very creative
working on different projects

Negative aspects
too busy
don't have time
travelling too much
restless
all over the place

Nine of Wands

The Nine of Wands represents breaking barriers. Here we have to learn to trust others or to delegate. We can't do it on our own, we have to allow people to give us a hand. A commander without soldiers cannot win the war!

You have to be prepared to accept the positive contribution which other people can make to your life. By allowing them to give, you will also be making them feel more positive about their lives as well. Other people need to give, as well as you.

Key words
generate trust
show people

Negative aspects
don't need anyone
refusing support
pride
feel weak

Ten of Wands

The Ten of Wands represents burdens. Here we are taking on board more than we can handle. We have allowed people to overburden us with their responsibilities or problems.

By the same token, there are times when it is worthwhile to carry such a burden: the long-term benefit may be considerable. But just plodding along in this way without any destination in sight is not.

Key words
devotion
don't get involved
obligation
pressure

Negative aspects
feeling obliged to carry burdens
trying to help too much

Page of Wands

The Page of Wands represents learning or travelling. Here we are approaching life philosophically. We are full of good intentions. On this road, we have much to learn about the spiritual aspect of life.

In this card, we are open-minded to new adventures. We are looking towards expanding our horizons. The Page takes us out on the road, back to the highway, i.e. the mainstream of life. Here we come back into contact with so many different influences; the effect is exciting. New people, new ideas, new possibilities, each offering to take us on a completely different journey!

This card is about confronting our limitations, and then expanding them.

Key words
games
reason
truth
human study

Negative aspects
wrong intention
too much effort
refusal to learn

Knight of Wands

The Knight of Wands represents a dynamic male energy. This card portrays the quality of being enthusiastic. This is the knight in shining armour ready to rescue the weak. He is forceful, extrovert and full of life.

He is an inspirational force which gives us a vision of how things might be better. With him, we feel that we can almost reach out and touch the exotic possibilities that he alludes to. He incites to action, to get moving!

Key words
vigilant
aggressive
lively
optimism
impatient
exploration

Negative aspects
macho
passionate
over imposing
impulsive

Queen of Wands

The Queen of Wands portrays an independent minded woman. She stands on her own two feet. She is strong and supportive. She doesn't wait to be told what to do. She likes her freedom of action and choices.

She is not going to wait around for things to happen to her; she will make them happen herself! She will instigate her own relationships, and if they don't work out, she will go it alone, clearing the decks of the unsuitable to make way for someone better to come along.

Key words

friendly

warmth

active

helping

initiator

guide

attractive

Negative aspects

too bossy

obstinate

King of Wands

The King of Wands represents a man of leadership and inspiration. He is a teacher figure. He guides, controls and directs.

Under his influence, some semblance of order is achieved – he encourages us to reach our full potential, he pushes us to our limits. He protects us, but expects our support in his battles as well. He is a tribal leader, bringing his people together under one banner, rallying us against suppression and towards freedom for us all.

Key words

force

responsible

power of command

management

Negative aspects
too domineering
dictatorial
rude

TWO

SPREADS

So far we have looked at the individual meanings of the cards, and how we can use them to empower ourselves in different ways. In this section we shall look at how the cards are set out in various patterns, and what the combined message of a set of cards might be.

You can pick out cards for yourself, or for others. It is difficult to be objective when laying out the cards for yourself, as you might want to hear a particular message and be unreceptive to other aspects of advice and guidance which the Tarot can offer. In laying the cards out for a friend, or someone who has asked you for a consultation, it is best if they are present with you, although it is possible to do readings for someone at a distance.

First, the cards are shuffled. If you are consulting the cards for yourself, stop the shuffling when you feel that the moment is 'right'. If someone else is shuffling, let them go on until they feel that they have shuffled enough. Only a few minutes will normally suffice; don't let them shuffle for much longer than that. If you are reading the cards for someone at a distance who wants a reading, e.g. over the telephone, ask them to tell you when to stop. Here, you are doing the mechanics of the actual shuffling, while it is they who stop the process; there is a synchronicity involved in determining which cards will come up in a reading.

Now, lay out the cards. There is no 'one way', or even 'best way' of doing this. The spreads below are suggestions, but ones which I think you will get a lot out of if you try them.

It is not possible to give the meanings of the cards as if they were frozen in stone, carved definitively for all time, for all people, and in all situations. An individual card will shift in its meaning for you; at one point in your life it will refer more to one thing than another. It will reflect back what you need to know, depending on where you are in your Journey at the moment of seeking reference.

What you will find in this section is what those basic meanings are, but allowing some element of flexibility in how you approach them and in what you take from them. Otherwise you will be limiting yourself in terms of what you are going to be able to come away with.

In working with the Tarot, you will be raising issues in your life; issues such as personal independence or commitments will tend to surface and demand that you confront the underlying causes of related problems. If the weak link in the chain of your life concerns money, then the Tarot will force you to confront your financial difficulties and get a handle on them. If the weak link in your life is to do with, for example, love, relationships, partners, family, children, parents, self-worth or valuing others, then the Tarot will force your attention into that area, or combination of areas. It can be rather disturbing to find one's life, previously arranged in tidy little boxes with labels neatly stuck on, suddenly in disarray and in a state of upheaval. Wherever the upheaval takes place – stay with it. A process of cleansing must occur before the underlying negative conditions can be successfully removed and a more permanent condition of happiness realised. An analogy which is useful on this point would be having a painful tooth – if any remedial treatment is too late it is better to have the tooth yanked out in one painful moment than to have to suffer the insistent agony of it sitting there indefinitely, flaring up over and over again.

This is not to say that negative things must inevitably happen when you begin any kind of self-developmental work; but it does mean that you must be prepared to let go of some of your negative patterns before you can begin to embrace life differently. Before the cup of your life can be filled with the new wine of life's experiences, it must first of all be emptied of the old wine. In the Tarot, the symbol of the cup is an important one – what it symbolises is our ability to receive – how can we receive any new experiences and new opportunities for growth and fulfilment, if the cups which we carry in our hands are filled already?

Self-development needn't be traumatic – it can be more upsetting to try to carry all of the garbage of the past with us. Often all that is required is that we be prepared to let go of the feelings of bitterness, remorse, lost opportunity, to find that the solutions which we have been looking for all along are sitting there under our very noses, and have been all along.

The Tarot in this regard is a servant – but it is not your master. It is not a judge, dominating your life. It is not there to tell you that you have been good or bad; although some people approach the Tarot in this way. It is almost like a replay of when we were children and would approach our parents, expecting a reprimand, or hoping for approval. The Tarot can give us specific advice, although it is there primarily as a mirror; and it will reflect back a version – or a vision – of what each person staring into it needs to see. As with any mirror, there will always be factors influencing the extent to which any such experience is 'accurate', i.e. bears a resemblance to the reality of the person seeking its insight. In some cases, the querent will find that the message they receive from the experience rings true, and is a confirmation of things which they have instinctively known anyway, but needed confirmation from an unbiased source. At other times any such consultation will throw up issues which the querent may feel have already been dealt with, or which are no longer relevant, or 'live issues'. The Tarot may well be telling them that they have not truly dealt with the past, and are merely hiding from it by putting their feelings 'on hold'. It is for each person to receive what they will, and what they can, from their own personal experience with the Tarot. It is not for anyone to force their opinions on others, and in this respect it is possible that the professional Tarot reader can easily make the mistake of slipping from the role of ship's navigator, to ship's captain, setting aside the responsibility of the individual for taking control of their own life. The Tarot is a gentle energy – it can only ever suggest, and never insist that the querent take something on board and act upon it. The Tarot does not always show what is actually happening in someone's life – it will more often tend to show what needs to be done by the querent, by high-lighting a particular area and bringing the querent to the point where those issues can be looked at – and hopefully successfully resolved.

Keep it Simple

In working your way through a spread in a reading, go systemati-cally at first, until you get the feel of how it all fits together. Remember that there may be inconsistencies in what seems to be showing in the spread; on the one hand this may well be because people's lives are riddled with inconsistencies and contradictions. On the other hand, you will have to learn how to 'fine tune' your readings to make it all fit together.

Be intuitive, and don't try to apply the meanings of each card liter-ally, or 'by the book'. Try to get a more 'general' feeling of each card, and let that sense guide you through the spread. Remember also that the art of Tarot readership might take a bit of time to perfect; although it can be learnt in a short space of time, as with anything else it might take you a while to really become comfortable with it.

So, don't let any hidden standard which you might feel you have to live up to make you feel overly critical about your achievements!

Above all, keep it simple!

The Triadic Spread

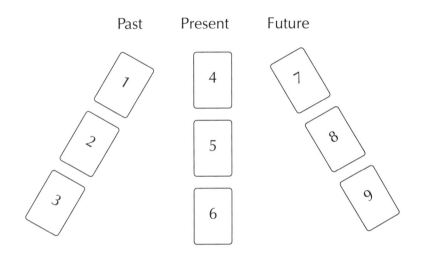

The Triadic Spread

This is a very simple spread, in which the cards you lay out on the left will represent the past, those in the middle the present, and those on the right the future. You can lay out as many cards as you wish on either stack, and elucidate as far as you wish, but it is best to keep it to three in each stack, at least until you get the hang of it. This symbol was used by the ancient Druids, and shows the rays of the sun descending to earth. Thus it is a symbol of teaching, and enlightenment.

139

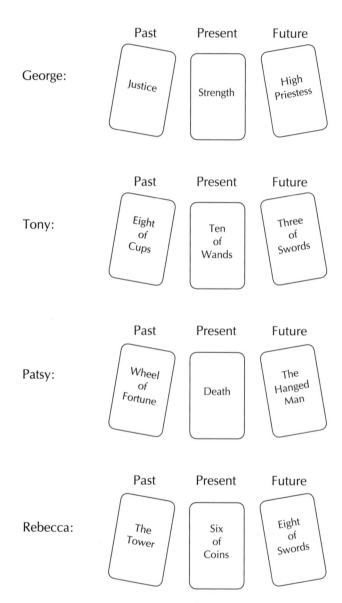

George:

Past | Present | Future

Justice | Strength | High Priestess

Tony:

Past | Present | Future

Eight of Cups | Ten of Wands | Three of Swords

Patsy:

Past | Present | Future

Wheel of Fortune | Death | The Hanged Man

Rebecca:

Past | Present | Future

The Tower | Six of Coins | Eight of Swords

Sample spreads

Opposite, we have some sample spreads for you to practise linking the cards together. Be experimental. In a live reading, if you want to know more about the person's past, present or future, get them to pick more cards and lay them down on the part of the spread which pertains to that time period, and it will tell you more.

With this technique you can keep opening up the other person's life. You can keep going until you feel you have done enough.

Imagine you have these people in front of you. Look through your deck and pick out the cards we have given in these examples, and then put them into place in the way we have shown. Start reading what is shown there.

The Celtic Cross

1   *The general situation*

2   *The general situation in more detail*

3   *On the person's mind*

4   *The influences of the last three years*

5   *The influences of the last year*

6   *The influences of the coming year*

7   *Doorway from the present to the future*

8   *Personal life*

9   *Hopes or anxieties*

10   *The overview – the 'by the way'*

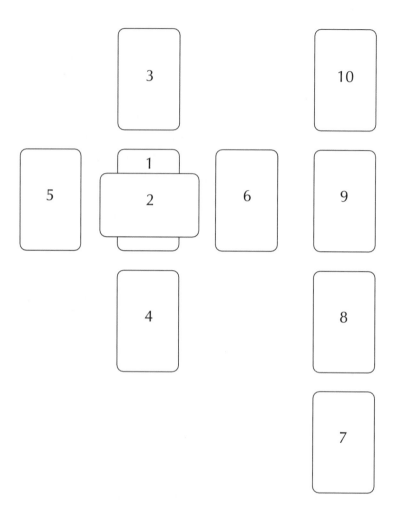

The Celtic Cross

This spread is good for looking at someone else's life, although it is not quite so useful in looking at your own.

The first two cards show different aspects of the present situation. The third card shows us what is on the querent's mind. The fourth gives us an idea of what the influence of the last three years or so has been. It is also the 'base' of the cross, where it rests upon the ground, and therefore what is the actual foundation of the querent's situation. The fifth card shows us the last six months to one year, although it can show even more recent influences than that. The sixth card shows us the influences of the year ahead, while the seventh represents the doorway from the present into the future – in other words, how the querent moves from his present situation into the future influences. Whereas the sixth card tends to show what will be happening to the querent from external sources, this card shows what he needs to do in order to maximise the benefits he will receive from them. The eighth card shows us not so much 'the final situation', but really provides us with an overview, as well as raising some issues not addressed in cards one to nine; a kind of 'any other business' item at the bottom of the agenda of any committee meeting. The first nine cards hang together, while the tenth is really the beginning of a new chain of interpretation.

In order to 'open up' this spread, you can either get the querent to pick out additional cards or just deal them straight off the top of the stack over the relevant card in the basic spread, taking the symbolism to relate to the area for which you require greater elucidation. You can use this enhancing technique either to answer specific questions, or because you require more information than the basic ten cards are coming up with.

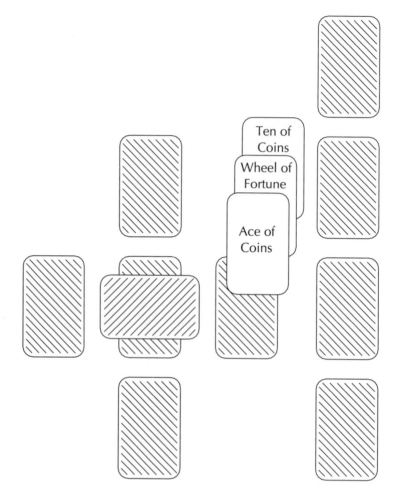

Enhancing Technique

Sample spread

In this example the querent's name is Simon. These are his cards:

		Judge- ment
	Wheel of Fortune	

Death

Five of Wands	Ten of Swords	Seven of Wands	Ace of Coins

	Queen of Swords		Two of Coins

		The Empress

1 **Death** *'This shows a clearing process, a time in your life when certain things may well be stripped away. The Death card, by the way, doesn't indicate that you or anyone else is going to die. It is a time of endings, so that new beginnings can begin to occur.*

2   **Ten of Swords** *'This card crossing Death
      shows that this period is particularly
      difficult. Together these cards would
      suggest a heavy time for you – there is a
      sense of loneliness which is very strong – a
      feeling of you being alone in a world which
      doesn't care. Depression is shown by these
      two cards together: you are going through
      a long dark tunnel, and there is a feeling of
      being almost lost in a great labyrinth.*

3   **The Wheel** *'On your mind we have the
      Wheel, which is a hopeful card. It shows
      that even though the objective conditions
      through which you are passing are difficult,
      you have in mind a number of hopes and
      aspirations which are keeping you going.
      Your vision of the future is basically
      hopeful; you have high expectations about
      the future, and it is this innate sense of
      cheerfulness which is sustaining you
      through your present adversity.*

4   **Queen of Swords** *'If we look at the
      influence of the slightly more distant past,
      in this card we see your relationships with
      women represented here. It shows a
      background influence of trouble with
      women, and difficulties you have had in
      forming close relationships. In a sense, this
      has actually helped you, as it has given you
      a determination to achieve fulfilment*

without being reliant on emotional happiness. Instead of swimming in relationships, you have developed the momentum to become successful in other ways, particularly through the world of action, where you can achieve recognition and success on your own merits.

5   **Five of Wands** *'This card shows me that over the last year or so you have gone into something which is particularly competitive, something which has taxed your abilities to the maximum, and brought you not necessarily into conflict with others, but into situations in which your abilities have been pitted in the marketplace against theirs.*

6   **Seven of Wands** *'The Seven of Swords in your near future indicates that both emotionally and professionally the coming period will be even more competitive: the advantage is that you will be able to bring into these situations all the skills in conflict which you have acquired over the last year. My advice to you is that you should be careful not to overcommit yourself, not to stretch yourself too far beyond your own limitations. You should approach these challenges step by step, jumping over the hurdles with which you are faced one by one, rather than facing them all at once. In this way you will win the race.*

7   **The Empress** *'Your seventh card is the
     Empress, which comes up a lot for those
     who are developing their creative skills.
     Writers, actors, artists, etc, tend to get this
     card. It shows that over the coming period
     you will be bringing to fruition your skills,
     and your abilities will have an excellent
     chance to manifest. Even emotionally, you
     will find that relationships become a lot
     smoother, more harmonious under this
     influence. With this card in your strategic
     seventh place, people will be more readily
     drawn to you. Offers of work and
     invitations to love will also come
     more easily.*

8   **Two of Coins** *'In this place, the Two of
     Coins shows a move from where you are
     currently living, and that this move will
     continue, being connected with your work
     life. You will be on the move professionally
     as well, going through a number of
     different positions, making many new
     contacts which you will be able to build
     upon later.*

9   **Ace of Coins** *'This shows a big doorway
     opening up for you. This is in the place of
     your hopes and aspirations. Because it is so
     closely placed to the Two of Coins (beneath)
     and Judgement (above) it is given a greater
     degree of objectivity than if it were*

*surrounded by more 'airy' or 'watery'
cards. So this isn't just something which
you are hoping for. This is something to
which the cards are assigning a greater
degree of reality.*

10   **Judgement** *'This card shows that in the
coming period, your life will be going
through a major transformation. You will
quite possibly complete the cycle of this
transformation by actually going abroad,
where I feel your Ace of Coins and Two of
Coins will be taking you. In any case, the
whole of your life will have totally changed
within the twelve month cycle being looked
at in this spread.'*

Feedback from Simon

It turns out that Simon is an actor, and that he has only recently left
drama school. His relationships with women have traditionally been
bad, and about a year ago he broke up with his girlfriend, who had
come to the conclusion that he was a dreamer, a 'no hoper'. Over
the last year he has tried to find work as an actor, but has only been
able to find bar work and waitering. When he came for the reading
he was on the verge of giving up and going back to his hometown
to work with his father in the family business.

Resolution: He will keep bashing away at his new profession, and
see what comes of it. As a result of the reading he will not give up,
but will weather the storm that he is going through with a renewed
sense of determination, taking it more in his stride now that he can
see that it is going to lead somewhere.

Two years later

Simon's acting career took a new turn when he moved flat. He was introduced to a new agent who saw his potential, and who subsequently booked him for a national tour in a pantomime. This in turn led to him meeting other contacts, after which he was booked for a top London show. He is currently deciding which of a number of top international contracts he should sign up for. Relationships of a more personal nature still haven't produced what is destined to be the great love of his life, but as Simon has become more fulfilled as a person, so in turn others have found him to be less miserable and more attractive to be around.

This is an actual example of a reading (in a slightly abbreviated form) which I did quite a while back (although his name has been changed). He is actually very famous now, and often appears on national television. And he still comes to me for readings.

Note: As you go through the reading with someone, you can verify with them that what you are saying is making sense. Sometimes they might have difficulty placing everything you have to say, but it should ultimately connect with what is actually going on in their life.

If you run dry at any stage, you can always use the enhancing technique outlined above.

The Astrological Spread

*1st House (Aries and Mars) Basic personality:
psychological motivation, personal qualities,
disposition and temperament.*

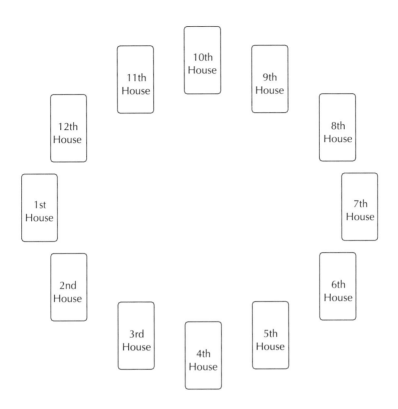

The Astrological Spread

2nd House (Taurus and Venus) Possessions: work, personal worth, values. Attitudes towards security, possessions and partners.

3rd House (Gemini and Mercury) Communication: brothers, sisters, relatives, early education, environment, transport.

4th House (Cancer and the Moon) Domestic life: home, mother.

5th House (Leo and the Sun) Love life: creativity, pleasure, children, love affairs, amusement.

6th House (Virgo and Mercury) Work life: routine work, health, diet exercise, hobbies.

7th House (Libra and Venus) One to one relationships: partnerships, marriage, contracts.

8th House (Scorpio and Pluto) Major changes: sex, inheritance, investment, other people's resources.

9th House (Sagittarius and Jupiter) Learning: higher education, long-distance travel, ideals, dreams, challenge, beliefs, philosophy.

10th House (Capricorn and Saturn) Achievements: aspirations, ambitions, careers, father.

11th House (Aquarius and Uranus) Social life: objectives, friends.

12th House (Pisces and Neptune) Mystical life: seclusion, escapism, faith, institutions.

This spread is a bit more complicated than the others, but try it out – it can give a deeper perspective. It works on the basis of the twelve astrological houses, although you do not need any prior knowledge of astrology in order to use it. This spread is good for looking at your own life, and also those of others, who may or may not be present. The cards should be placed in an anti-clockwise direction, from the 1st House to the 12th House.

The Tree of Life Spread

1   *Neptune: Individual relationship with infinity/spirit/god.*

2   *Uranus: Revolutionary change, influence, inventiveness.*

3   *Saturn: Sense of limitation, lessons, disciplines, responsibilities.*

4   *Jupiter: Area in which blessings manifest, optimism, positivity.*

5   *Mars: Area of combat, personal battles.*

6   *Sun: Personal development, growth through life.*

7   *Venus: Creative, artistic area, harmony, accord.*

8   *Mercury: Communication, how one is learning, studying.*

9   *Moon: Intuition, psychic abilities.*

10   *Earth: Physical universe, real and tangible experiences.*

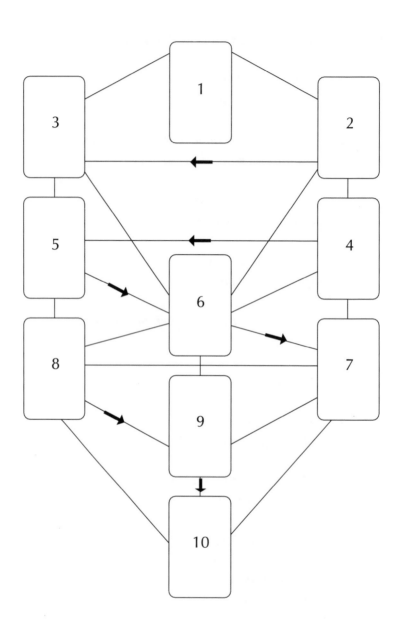

The Tree of Life Spread

Here you lay out the cards in the pattern shown. Each card epitomises the influence of one of the Spheres of the Tree, which represents an area of your life and the work confronting you in it. This spread is deeply mystical, is ideal for looking at your own life, and should be consulted rarely. Some say it should only be done once in your life.

The Crossroads Spread

This is an excellent spread to use in a dilemma – when you are at a crossroads in your life. If you have two specific courses of action open to you, you should consult this spread.

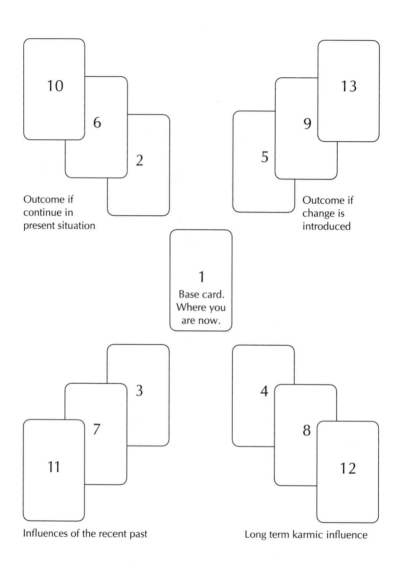

10

6

2

Outcome if
continue in
present situation

13

9

5

Outcome if
change is
introduced

1
Base card.
Where you
are now.

3

7

11

Influences of the recent past

4

8

12

Long term karmic influence

The Crossroads Spread

The Chakra Spread

1   Base: Foundations of life: material
     conditions

2   Sacral: Sexuality, life force, creative
     potential

3   Solar plexus: Needs, energy, willpower

4   Heart: Love, harmony, synthesis

5   Throat: Communication, expression,
     contact with others

6   Brow: Psychic realm, visualisation,
     awareness level

7   Crown: Connection with the world of spirit,
     ability to draw down power

This spread approaches the Querent's life from a strongly
spiritual/karmic viewpoint.

The Relationship Spread

This spread is great for looking at any relationship – but especially
where you and the other person are connected with love and/or
desire.

1   What you are bringing into the
     relationship.

The Relationship Spread

2   *Where you are now, in relation to the other person.*

3   *What you are hoping to get from the relationship.*

4   What the other person is bringing into
      their relationship with you.

5   What they are getting out of it.

6   What they are hoping to achieve/experience
      with you.

7   How you see the other person.

8   How they see you.

9   How you saw him/her when you first.

10   How the other person saw you on your
      first meeting.

11   Your own anxieties/unconscious fears.

12   The other person's anxieties/unconscious
      fears.

13   External influences upon you.

14   External influences upon the other person.

15   Where the relationship will go.

This spread is amazing in its ability to reveal incredible things about any relationship which you may be involved in – or just about to get involved in. I have been stunned at times at what this one has shown me.

Sample spread

Lucia comes to you for a reading. After she shuffles the cards, you lay them out in the format of the relationship spread. This is what you see:

1   Five of Cups

2   Two of Cups

3   Ten of Cups

4   The Hierophant

5   Seven of Swords

6   Nine of Cups

7   Knight of Cups

8   Eight of Wands

9   Emperor

10   Two of Coins

11   Eight of Swords

12   High Priestess

13   Four of Coins

14   Ten of Coins

15   Temperance

Now, don't panic! This looks a lot more complicated than it actually is. Let's go through this spread, step by step, working out how these cards might pertain to this woman's life.

'With the Five of Cups indicating what you are bringing into this relationship, it seems that you carry with you a strong sense of disillusionment from a previous relationship. This past experience has on the one hand made you a bit wary of getting involved emotionally, and on the other hand, it has created a slight desperation that the person you have recently met is going to turn out to be "Mr Right".

'The Two of Cups suggests that there is a great deal of harmony in this relationship, and that the prospects seem to be quite good for the long term.

'What you are hoping to get out of this is the Ten of Cups, i.e. either marriage, or a very long-term sense of emotional commitment.

'Looking at what the other person is bringing with him, we see the Hierophant. Since one of the meanings of this card is orthodoxy, it suggests that this person is from a conventional background, and for him this relationship may be something that is outside his normal range of experience. Another aspect of this card is teaching; possibly this person has experienced his past relationship(s) as a learning process.

'He is experiencing his relationship with you as the Seven of Swords. I am not sure whether he is making particular sacrifices to be with you, or whether part of him feels that his time with you is "stolen" in some way. One aspect of this card is that it shows something happening surreptitiously. Is his relationship with you secret in some way? (At this point it turns out that he is in fact married.)

'The Nine of Cups shows that what he will get out of the relationship is a good time, but he may not want to give you the kind of commitment that you are looking for. He may not see you as quite the permanent feature in his life as you would like.

'You see him as the Knight of Cups, in other words as an emotionally very receptive man with whom you can relate in an emotional way.

'He sees you as the Eight of Wands, which is a card indicating a high energy level, with much action. It suggests passion, but a passion which might be shortly moving on to something – or someone – else.

'When you first met him you saw him as the Emperor, as someone who epitomised strength, power and independence. It was these qualities which greatly attracted you towards him.

'When he first met you, he saw you as the Two of Coins. This is a card of transition, so he saw you as someone who was in transit at the time. This may well mean that you were passing through his life at the time, and that he had to act quickly in order to attract you, before you moved on to something else.

'Your own unconscious anxieties are shown in the Eight of Swords, which in this case shows a fear of being by-passed, or of being outside the mainstream of the river of life, and therefore of love.

'His fears are shown in the High Priestess – part of him is a bit afraid that you might well turn out to be something more significant to him than he has taken you for so far.

'The Four of Coins is the external influence upon you. It is a card which shows security, not necessarily materially, but as you can see from the picture on the card, it shows someone grasping at what has come their way. Thus, your own need for emotional reassurance and security is particularly strong.

'The Ten of Coins is indicating his anxieties. Part of him fears that his relationship with you could well undermine his family and home life. What has started as a fling for him could well turn out to be a great deal more, with consequences he hadn't banked on.

'Temperance is the card showing where the relationship will go. It is a card which means maturity, thus indicating that both of you will be going through some rather hard knocks as your relationship develops. However, it is likely that there will be some kind of continuing bond between you. You will learn a great deal from your relationship with each other. Another aspect of this card pertains to healing. It would seem that the two of you may well be able to help heal each other's wounds from the past whilst together. In your case, Lucia, addressing your need for emotional security, while in his case, dealing with his need for greater emotional freedom outside his marriage, family life and orthodox lifestyle.'

Feedback from Lucia

It turned out that she had met a man with whom she had become involved, at first only sexually but later emotionally as well. It later transpired that he was married, and hadn't anticipated getting emotionally involved as well. As a result of the reading Lucia was able to confront him, whereupon he admitted that he had no intention of leaving his wife. Lucia was able to adjust her expectations of the relationship, and with the greater honesty that she had been able to bring to bear, found that her relationship with him had moved into the realm of friendship and affinity that she had never before experienced with a man. She continued seeing him, but had overcome her immediate response of seeing him as the romantic answer to all her problems.

Tips on Tarot Reading for Others

The main categories which you will be expected to cover in a reading are:

1   *Money: investments, savings, gambles*

2   *Ambitions: potentials, secret desires, ambitions*

3   *Career: job change/title change, advancement, conflicts within workplace*

4   *Love life/sex life: remember that these two are rarely the same*

5   *Expectations: dreams, fantasies, predictions*

6   *Health: positive as well as negative influences*

7   *Travel: short and long journeys, people returning from the past, business trips, tourism*

To read the cards for someone else is a big responsibility. You must be careful what you say to others, and aware of the possible implications of your reading.

1   *Articulate clearly and don't mumble – some people have hearing difficulties.*

2   *Allow the querent to ask questions. By answering their questions you can more effectively personalise the reading.*

3   *Avoid negative predictions. Someone who is troubled by worries or has had disappointment in life needs a boost to their self-esteem, a greater belief in themselves.*

4   *Agree with your querent's views. Most people actually know the answers to their problems. They merely need some emotional support.*

5   *Advise your querent in a common-sense way. Most people, you will find, are interested in practical alternatives to their problems.*

6   *You can feel free to move between past, present and future as you go through the cards.*

7   *Provide the querent with something positive to look forward to, a light at the end of the tunnel. Remember that they have the power to make it happen.*

8   *A push in the right direction is all most people need. Predictions of doom and gloom nobody needs. But show them how they can avoid the bad as well.*

9   *Absorb the mood of the querent. Let yourself feel their fears, their hopes, share in their dreams. This way you will start functioning as a psychic, as an intuitive person. You will come to see and understand so much more this way.*

10   *Believe in your predictions, or don't predict. Be authentic – don't be trapped into making things up just for the sake of having something interesting to say.*

11   *Befriend your querent. You will be remembered by them positively in years to come if you do.*

12   *Don't get drawn into casting spells or curses. Bring mystery into the reading by all means: that's a vital part of it, but don't compound your querent's problems with scary supernatural rubbish. They have come to you for help.*

13   Bewitch, bedazzle, baffle, by all means, but
      in moderation. Like the seasoning used in
      food, a little goes a long way.

14   Do be careful of predictions regarding
      health and legal matters. These things are
      best left in the hands of professionals.
      Remember, you wouldn't want the local
      doctor to start doing tarot readings in
      competition with you, would you? So let
      him do his thing, and you can do yours.

15   Balance the reading – look at love, career,
      family, all the areas of human concern. If
      you miss out one you might just miss
      the area that is actually of interest to
      the querent.

16   Blend your statements into a story format.
      Don't give the impression that you are
      delivering a staccato-like string of isolated
      statements. This is awful.

17   You can ask the querent's birthday, and
      comment on its astrological significance,
      if you have enough knowledge of the
      different signs.

18   Build up your querent's self-esteem
      and ego. If you can boost someone's
      self-confidence, they will consider their
      money/time well spent.

19   Your querent must be able to judge the
      accuracy of your reading on the basis of
      what they know to be true.

20   If you want to charge a fee, do so, as long
      as you feel that what you are offering is
      going to be worth the money you are
      charging. Alternatively, get the querent
      to bring you a bottle of wine, some home-
      made pies: anything, as long as there is
      something by way of exchange. Just doing
      freebies will tire you out and your readings
      will become thin and dispirited as a result.

21   Create a comfortable atmosphere where
      you are doing the reading. You don't have
      to deck out the room like a Hollywood film
      set, but you can make it pleasant.

22   Constantly plant positive seeds – most
      predictions become self-fulfilling. The
      querent will make it come out that way.

23   Clarify predictions: be specific if you can.
      You can be guided by the questions you are
      asked, allowing your answers to become
      increasingly specific.

24   Don't underestimate the intelligence of the
      other person. If you try to bluff, they will
      spot it. Just be as honest as you can.
      Be yourself.

25   *Select a style of reading that suits you. Don't
      model your reading style on somebody
      else's. If you do this it will sound unnatural.*

26   *Channel intuitive information to your
      querent as part of the reading. Don't be
      afraid of being intuitive. You may be
      surprised at what comes out. Afterwards,
      you will be thinking, 'Where did that
      come from?'*

About Reversed Cards

By reversed cards we mean cards that come out upside down when
you lay them out. Some people attach more significance to this than
others. In fact it varies as to how much significance should be placed
on cards that come out in this way. There are no rigid rules, but basi-
cally a reversed card might mean a delay, a mitigation, an insuffi-
cient or conversely an excessive quality to the meaning of the card.
It just puts more of a question mark over the meaning of the card
in the place where you find it. But don't get stumped by it!

It is possible to get very mechanistic and dogmatic in interpreting
the cards, almost as if one were deciphering ancient Egyptian hiero-
glyphics. Reading the cards isn't really like this: it's more like pad-
dling a boat downstream. You have to keep in view the person's life,
and make sure that the cards fit into it, and not the other way round.
When you start using your intuitive aspect you will be able to set
aside the exact meanings of the cards and go by feelings as well. It
is not one thing or the other here; it is a question of using both in

order to do an effective reading.

So even if a card is reversed, don't immediately jump to the 'opposite' meaning. For example, if you have the Three of Swords reversed, it doesn't mean that the querent is heart-broken. It would probably mean that he/she has suppressed a lot of feelings, and that these will need a lot of help in being released. If the querent has the Wheel of Fortune reversed, it doesn't mean a lack of abundance but, more likely, an overly optimistic attitude and, therefore, the need to look more carefully at the small print of any agreements or deals which they might be getting into. It would point more to the fact that the querent *feels* unduly lucky, rather actually *being* lucky.

The Court Cards

These tend to show either different aspects of the querent, or the tapestry of personalities surrounding him. Significant people might therefore be shown taking on a role either in his personal life, at work, in the family, and so on. Sometimes the court cards show situations. For example, the Queen of Wands might show the kind of women the querent is attracted to, or with whom he goes through a repeat pattern of some kind. Falling in a man's spread it could even show an aspect of himself, i.e. that part of his personality which is innovative but still receptive to the inspirations of others. Similarly, the King of Coins falling in a woman's spread could show that aspect of her personality which is supportive, masculine, able to initiate on the material or physical level.

Long gone are all the old associations between the court cards and 'dark-haired women' or 'blond, blue-eyed men'. This link may have been relevant at one time, but the world has changed since those times, and so have the meanings of the cards. These days, anyone can change the colour of their hair overnight; with special contact lenses they can even change the colour of their eyes. The cards have more important things to do, more important messages to deliver than people's colouring.

Just as the world in which we live continues to change, so will the tarot, because it is a living, vibrant thing, not some static, unchangeable formula preserved in vinegar.

When reading the cards for gays or lesbians, you can be aware that a masculine card in a female's spread might more especially indicate a dynamic aspect of her sexuality, just as a feminine card in a man's spread could indicate a receptive aspect of his sexuality. Again, while there are guidelines, the tarot is something which is a bit different for each person, and there are no cast-iron rules. You are mostly going to learn through direct experience, which means you finding out for yourself.

Timing

Some tarot readers have tried to find a way of determining the time when such and such will happen. This is, in my experience, very difficult. What we are looking at in the tarot is a person's karma. There is no system of using the cards to determine when something might occur. Some books suggest that if you turn over a card in answer to a question like this, and you see a number six, for example, this might show six months, six weeks or six years. This isn't a lot of use ultimately. You can't just take the number on the card and use it to gauge when something will happen.

You may get an intuitive flash, but you may not. Don't get pressurised into putting a time limit on something which you know in

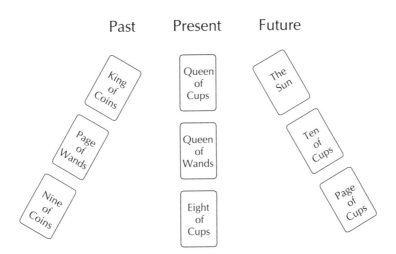

your heart is not likely. Sometimes the pressure from a querent can be quite considerable, which is understandable when you think about how frustrating it must be to be told something but then not to have an 'expected time of arrival' given as well.

Exercises

You may like to try the following readings on 'dummy' querents, to assess your progress. Lay out the appropriate cards from your own deck, and make it sound as real as possible. Don't look for the answers at the back of the book – you are providing your own!

Past   Present   Future

King of Coins   Queen of Cups   The Sun

Page of Wands   Queen of Wands   Ten of Cups

Nine of Coins   Eight of Cups   Page of Cups

Steve just wants a general reading. He has never had a tarot reading before.

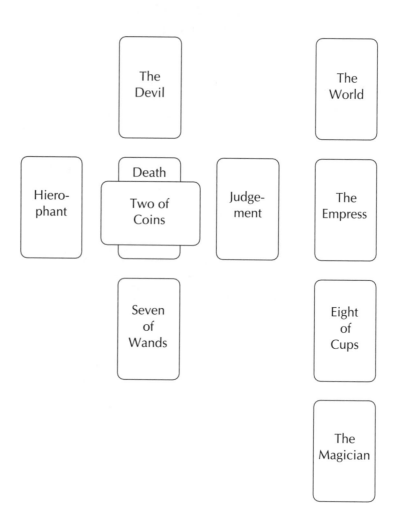

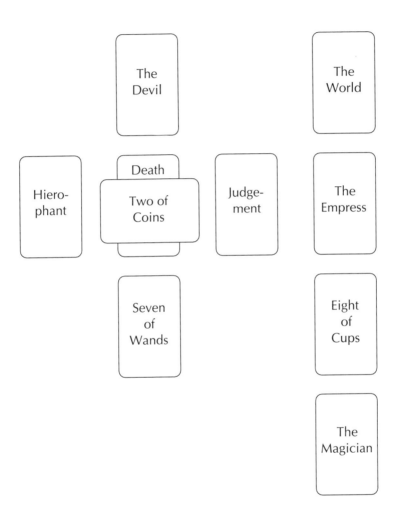

Fred has just been made redundant. What should he do?

The
Devil

The
World

Hiero-
phant

Death

Two of
Coins

Judge-
ment

The
Empress

Seven
of
Wands

Eight
of
Cups

The
Magician

Sophie is a literary agent and is unsure about taking on a new client. What do the cards suggest?

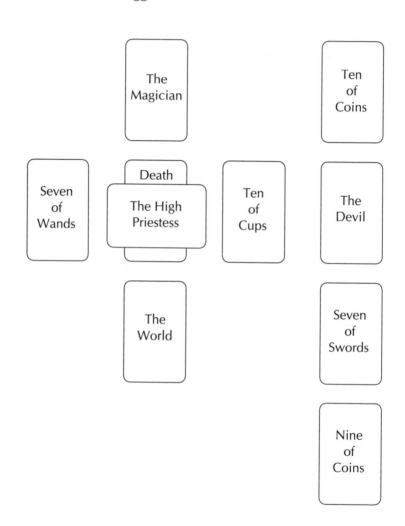

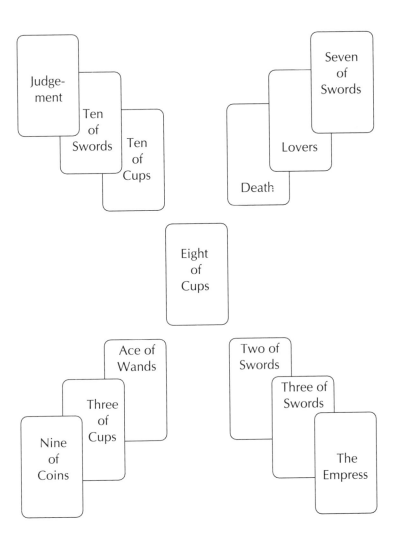

Susan has a choice to make between two lovers. Which path should she choose?

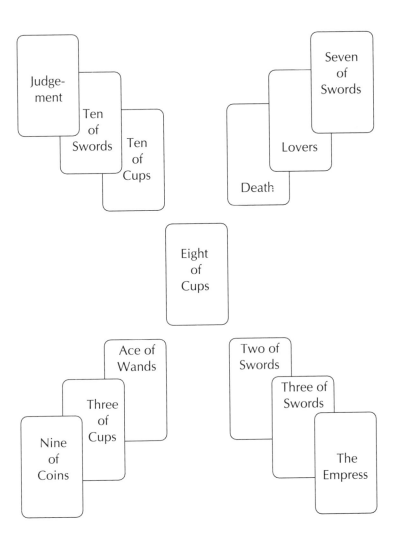

Sarah is thinking about giving up her job and going freelance. What do her cards have to say?

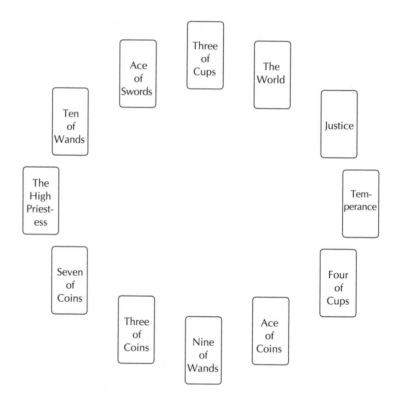

John has just met Karla. What are the prospects for a relationship between them?

John		Karla

Ten of Swords

Ace of Wands

Eight of Coins — Three of Wands — High Priest-ess

Eight of Cups — Two of Coins — Five of Cups

Three of Swords

Lovers

Strength

Justice

The Star

The Tower

Judgement

THREE

MEDITATION
With the Tarot

The Value of Meditation

We are all looking for happiness. We may search from one relation-ship to another in order to find it. We may alternatively immerse ourselves acquiring material objects, or we may go to the other extreme and try to find happiness through helping others in need. In themselves, there is nothing wrong with any of these orienta-tions, but they cannot give us what we are looking for at the bottom of all these things. We experience heartbreak when the relationship around which we have based our lives becomes redundant; we feel dejected and lost when our usefulness in any field of work is over and we are faced with the sack; when our friends, children, etc move on we feel a sense of mourning.

The teaching of the tarot is that there is a sense of lasting happiness which everyone can achieve. The purpose of the tarot isn't – and never really was – to just predict likely outcomes from existing situ-ations, but rather to show how each of us can live more fulfilling lives regardless of whether, for example, we work a sixty-hour week, are raising children single-handed or living in a city.

By practising the wisdom of the tarot, we can learn to be happy in almost any situation, even those which our minds tell us are difficult or unacceptable. At the centre of the tarot we have teachings which show us how we can move away from fear, anxiety, anger, and, through realisation and self-development, resolve our internal con-tradictions so as to achieve a state of serenity in our daily lives.

In meditation we are consciously directing our mental processes from one state to another, say, from desire to love. There are many forms of meditation. One form can involve staring fixedly at an object, either external to the body, or internally, as in a meditation on some personal problem. Its aim is to peel back the layers of the outer world by awakening a very subtle level of consciousness.

It is important to go at your own pace, and not try to force yourself to conform to some hidden standard of what you 'should' be experiencing as you go into these meditations.

This is just a general guideline for you. As you 'get into' these meditations you will increasingly know – without knowing where this knowledge has come from – what you should be doing.

In order to meditate on the right cards, once you have found what element you should be meditating on, pick out the appropriate suit, and pick out a card, or selection of cards which 'stands out'. For instance, if you feel that there isn't enough love in your life, pick out the Ace of Cups and/or the Two of Cups. Stand these cards on the table or mantelpiece in front of you and let your mind wander over the pictures shown in them. Don't look for any instant 'results' – they won't come to you that way. Instead, relax with whatever the pictures are showing you. In time, you will absorb the teaching and the guidance which the card(s) have to offer you. Gradually, you will begin to draw into your life precisely what you are missing. Another example would be in the work area. If you cannot find the right kind of work for yourself then pick out, for example, the Ace of Coins. Set it up on the table in front of you, and just leave it. You don't have to stare at it, but just leave it there, and allow it to 'come to life', as it were. You can leave it for a few days, weeks, or months, even. But as it is there, it becomes a focal point for your mind, and little by little you will begin to draw down into your life the right kind of work for yourself. This may come about by some chance encounter, or by a 'prompting' from life itself for you to move in a different direction.

What to Do

Sit down with your cards in your hands, flitting through the deck, and allow a particular card to 'stand out'. There may be something about the design of the card, or you may feel drawn to explore the realm of experience touched upon by this card for your session. Place the card down on the table in front of you.

There may be a set of cards – up to three or four, even, that you wish to explore more in depth. Lay them out in a small row in front of you, using something to prop them up from behind. You can light a candle at either side if you wish, and/or play some gentle or inspirational background music.

Ask yourself your reason for wishing to explore the realm suggested by your choice of card(s). Check on the thoughts which are beginning to run through your head. Don't be judgmental towards them. Don't cling on to any; similarly, don't push any away.

Now, take a much deeper breath than normal, and just allow your lungs to act as suction pumps; breathing in peace (the colour blue), and breathing out tension (the colour red). This will stabilise you throughout the length of the meditation.

Next, if you wish to investigate a particular topic, place your mind single-pointedly on that theme so that it becomes literally one with your own life experience. Let the scene shown in the card represent a major turning point in your life. Look upon the whole of your life experience in terms of the situation shown in the card. Maintain visual concentration on whatever the card is now beginning to show you. You may well find that the card is showing you a 'scene within a scene', and revealing something of its own inner significance to you.

183

At a certain point you may find yourself seeing something quite different within the card than normal vision was ever able to present to you. All this is quite 'normal'; what you are experiencing is the opening of a deeper sense of awareness. You may not be able to make sense of some of the imagery initially – but as your meditations progress you will find that your new-found sense of spiritual vision becomes more focused. Just as a new-born baby cannot 'make out' what it is seeing until some time after it is born, so with our sense of spiritual or 'psychic' vision do we find the same constraints applying.

Before you begin your session, it is important to read the meaning of the card(s), and get a good idea of what it means. Otherwise, you could go off on a tangent which has absolutely nothing to do with what the card actually represents.

At a certain point you may wish to close your eyes – it is entirely up to you how you want to run your sessions. While you are actually 'in session', though, it would be best to avoid referring to any book – even this one – until after you have actually finished. Above all, avoid having unrealistic expectations about how the session should go, or what you should be feeling, or coming away from the session with afterwards.

Each time you go into session, and 'enter' into any of the cards, you are actually creating a very positive energy, and enhancing your own level of awareness. It is important to carry this energy over into the 'real' world, so that some 'real' good may come of it. This energy is carried over from the meditative state to the realm of everyday activity as you move from meditation back into your 'normal' frame of mind. If you finish your session in an angry state of mind, or rush to finish it too quickly, a great deal of the positive energy is going to be lost.

Before you finish, just take a few minutes to recall your reasons and motivation for doing the meditation, and then direct your energy to the fulfilment of these same objectives. This will ensure that the act of dedication to these objectives takes place, and that you begin to experience real and positive benefits from your work.

It is also important to bring the fruits of your meditation into your everyday life.

As you progress in your meditations, become more aware of your impulsive reactions, and instead of following your thoughts and feelings blindly, watch your mind, be conscious, and attempt to deal with situations as skilfully as you possibly can. If you can bring this about, you are demonstrating success in your meditations on the tarot, and are actually evolving/developing positively.

During your meditations, your mind will tend to wander from one thing to the next, without any logical sequence. This is how the subconscious mind works, through association. Sometimes, you will get very excited, and your mind will begin to race ahead through a hundred and one forgotten memories, coming up with ideas, hopes, thoughts, realisations, resolutions, plans, expectations. Sometimes, it will throw up images that are very pleasing; other times it will show things that your mind has repressed, memories that you find difficult to deal with, and experiences which you have tried to clear from your mind. Even when the experiences are 'bad', they are still healing you. The negative experience has to be brought to the surface in order to be fully expiated; we each and every one of us have been through experiences which we subconsciously tie up into little knots and push down, down below the surface level of conscious awareness. But they must surface, and surface they will, like little bubbles floating upwards, only to be fully and finally dissipated

185

when they come back to your conscious level for the final time. Working with the tarot in this way, you will discover is a most powerful remedy, a therapeutic process second to none. However painful it may be, follow through with the meditation – a few tears now are better than carrying all that baggage for the next twenty years.

Visualisation is another excellent method: imagine a pale blue light entering through your head, flowing down through your abdomen, and back out through your feet. Concentrate on this experience as you go through it, visualising your body as a hollow container.

If you find yourself getting strange images or sensations, these are just normal reactions of the mind adjusting to the new activity of meditation which you have embarked upon. There is no cause for alarm. All you have to do here is simply observe whatever emotions or images occur around you, without trying to hold onto them, or without pushing them away, either. In time, they will dematerialise of their own accord. If any particularly disturbing experience continues over any length of time, or occurs with regularity, the best solution would probably be to discontinue with the meditations for a period until things have settled down.

Some people feel that they 'can't meditate', or that 'nothing is happening'. When this seems to be the case, recognise that it is going to take time to get you out of your old mental patterns, and that positive changes occur maybe more slowly at first, when change is occurring on a more fundamental level. The deeper the level of genuine change, the more slowly it actually manifests on an obvious level.

Sometimes, people who meditate on the tarot feel that their minds are actually getting more clogged up than they were before. (This is rather like washing clothes: before they can become clean, they must first of all get worse. As the washing process works, the water gets dirty, and it seems impossible to believe that the result will actually be a pile of sparkling white laundry. But it is part of the natural cycle of purification: once they have gone through the final rinse, the clothes are clean and ordered again.) Whenever I hear this response from my students, I tell them to have patience. So, similarly, I now say the same thing to you; there is a real need for patience and perseverance.

To help you develop a sense of perspective

Select a card which represents what your life might have been like if you had been born as an animal, or controlled by others in some way, constantly experiencing hunger, thirst and the fear of being killed. Let yourself 'drift' into the card, and look around to see what is going on about you. What sounds can you hear? What can you feel beneath your feet? Is it hot, or is it cold?

Inside this card now, visualise yourself as a beggar. Visualise yourself living in a totally repressive regime, where your every move is frowned upon, and where your best friends and loved ones are constantly disappearing. Let yourself become more 'solid' inside the card now, and imagine that you are suffering from some terrible disease, with each moment filled with pain.

Learn to appreciate the positive things in your life.

The next step is for you to look at what opportunities are open to you for you to live a fulfilled and meaningful life. Try and see the limitations of a lifestyle based around material objectives alone; look in detail at what kinds of love and friendship your life could be filled with. If you feel that your life could well do with some enhancement on a material level, visualise where (i.e. what country) you would like to live in; what kind of house, what kind of setting it would be in. Let your mind become very concentrated in visualising these images. You may not know how they may even begin to manifest in your life, but that in a sense is irrelevant; the material universe is like clay – it moulds itself around our thoughts – so rest assured that first of all a vision is needed. If people can't see an alternative for them in the future, then they won't be able to move towards that point.

Look at all these aspects slowly, without rushing through them. Within you is a far greater power than you ever expected; how now can you feel as though you can do anything other than succeed?

The tremendous energy and sense of power you will derive from these meditations will serve you well, if you first of all dedicate them to the well-being of all, and not just yourself.

Tarot meditation on friendship/conflict scenarios

Draw three cards from the deck; one for a friend, one for an 'enemy' – or at least someone who you have negative feelings towards – and the third for someone for whom your feelings are completely neutral. You may be drawn toward the court cards in this instance, or feel that other cards may more appropriately symbolise each of the characters in this meditation.

Place each of these cards in front of you.

Now look at the card representing your enemy; imagine that the person sitting inside that card is a man or woman who has harmed you in some way. Note the feelings of anger that arise within you. What could happen that might turn this person into a friend? Become aware of your feelings.

Next, look at the card to represent the stranger – imagine this person sitting inside the card; note your feelings towards this person – what situation could occur that would turn this person into a friend or an enemy? Note how fragile are relationships, and your feelings towards this character, and move on.

Now look at the card which you have chosen to represent your friend. Let yourself 'see' that person sitting inside that card. Remember that there was once a time before this person became your friend. Recognise that this friend might well move on in life – all friendships are in a state of flux. What could happen to make this same person into an enemy?

Now come back to the card which represents your enemy. Learn to feel differently about this person. Recognise that even one act of kindness could turn this person into something quite different from what you have experienced from them until now.

Let the faces and outlines of each of these three people become more distinct. Realise that each of these individuals can fulfil any of the three roles which your mind had selected for them and that they are each of them seeking happiness for themselves. It is only natural that we should feel closer to some people than to others, but recognise that no one is fixed unchangeably into any one category, unless it is by our own power of choice.

FOUR

WHERE TO GO
From Here

The tarot will be your really close companion on the trail that lies ahead. The insights which it gives you will always be useful, and we would encourage you to continue with your work. The more you help others, the more your own life will open up; the more you develop yourself, the more useful you will be to those around you.

You don't have to read a pile of books in order to understand something. You may want to read around the subject, though, and see what other people are saying about it. Feel free, by all means, but never let somebody else's theory become a substitute for your own realisation and wisdom.

The best way of continuing to develop is through helping others to do the same, so when you come across someone who is interested in finding out about the tarot, talk about your own experiences and share your knowledge. By meeting others, you will also have the opportunity to share their insights as well. However, some people have very strange ideas about what the tarot is, and what it can do, so don't let them force their opinions on you unless it is something which you want to believe.

Nevertheless, it would be a good idea to start linking up with people on the same wavelength as yourself; otherwise it is difficult for your interest to get the sort of nourishment which it will require in order to start blossoming. You may not see where you can go in order to find others on this wavelength, but just 'put it out there' in a positive frame of mind and they will start gravitating towards you. Don't let other people invalidate you, or minimise you, either with regard to your work with the tarot, or in any other respect in life, for that matter.

Here at the London Tarot Centre, we are in the process of putting together a network of tarot enthusiasts around the country, and eventually the world, in order to help facilitate the opening up of the wisdom of the tarot to even more people.

You may even wish to apply to train with us, in which case you are welcome to contact us at the address which is given at the end of this book.

APPENDIX

Evelyne Herbin is a highly experienced tarot reader and teacher. She is also a single mother who has devoted several years to raising her daughter Claudia. She is currently engaged in writing stories and self-awareness books for children and adults. Her main goal is to teach people how to be in control of their lives.

Terry Donaldson is also a highly experienced tarot practitioner and teacher who has developed his techniques over 20 years. He is founder and Director of the Tarot Training Centre and author of *The Lord of the Rings Tarot*, *Step-by-Step Tarot* and *The Dragon Tarot*.

The Tarot Training Centre

The Tarot Training Centre has been established to promote greater understanding of the Tarot. It runs in-house, one-to-one teaching and correspondence courses. Also tarot and astrological readings are available, either in person or over the phone.

Those interested in finding out more should contact:

For international promotions, and a wide spectrum of contacts.

The Tarot Training Centre

27 Psychic Mews
23 Queensway
London W2
Telephone: 020–7561–0345
e-mail: terrytarot@yahoo.com

Further Contacts

Australia
New Life Promotions (Australia)
Loched Bag 19
Pyrmont
NSW 2009
Telephone: 02–552–6833
Fax: 02–566–2354

United Kingdom
Festival for Mind, Body and Spirit
New Life Promotions
Arnica House
170 Campden Hill Road
London W8 7AS
Telephone: 020–7938–3788
Fax: 020–7723–7256

Mysteries
9/11 Monmouth Street
Covent Garden
London WC2H 9DA
Telephone: 020–7240–3688

For tarot decks, books, supplies, also tarot courses and readings. This shop is well worth a visit.

Thorsons
HarperCollins*Publishers*
77–85 Fulham Palace Road
Hammersmith
London W6 8JB
Telephone: 020–8741–7070
Fax 020–8307–4440

Thorsons publish a very wide
range of tarot decks and books,
as well as books on personal
development in general. Free
catalogue on request.

Watkins Bookshop
21 Cecil Court
Leicester Square
London WC2N 4EZ
Telephone: 020–7836–2182
Fax: 020–7836–6700

Has a very wide and famous
selection of second-hand and
hard-to-find books on the tarot,
and other related mystical
subjects.

David Westnedge Co.
5 Ferrier Street
London SW18 1SN
Telephone: 020–8871–2654
Fax: 020–8877–1241

For tarot decks and books.

USA
U.S. Games Systems Inc.
179 Ludlow Street
Stamford
CT 06902, USA
Telephone: 203–353–8400
Fax: 203–353–8431

For tarot decks, supplies and
books.

Taraco
PO Box 104
Sausalito
CA 94966–0104

Tarot Network News features
the latest on tarot contacts, new
developments, etc. Write to the
above address.

The Santa Cruz School for Tarot
and Qaballah Studies
Telephone: 408–423–9742.